University of Texas at Austin
Austin, Texas

Written by Erin Hall

Edited by Adam Burns, Meghan Dowdell, Kimberly Moore, Jon Skindzier, and Tim Williams

Layout by Meghan Dowdell

Additional contributions by Omid Gohari, Christina Koshzow, Christopher Mason, Joey Rahimi, and Luke Skurman

ISBN # 1-59658-013-5
ISSN # 1552-1796
© Copyright 2005 College Prowler
All Rights Reserved
Printed in the U.S.A.
www.collegeprowler.com

Last updated 9/27/05

Special thanks to: Babs Carryer, Andy Hannah, LaunchCyte, Tim O'Brien, Bob Sehlinger, Thomas Emerson, Andrew Skurman, Barbara Skurman, Bert Mann, Dave Lehman, Daniel Fayock, Chris Babyak, The Donald H. Jones Center for Entrepreneurship, Terry Slease, Jerry McGinnis, Bill Ecenberger, Idie McGinty, Kyle Russell, Jacque Zaremba, Larry Winderbaum, Roland Allen, Jon Reider, Team Evankovich, Lauren Varacalli, Abu Noaman, Jason Putorti, Mark Exler, Daniel Steinmeyer, Jared Cohon, Gabriela Oates, David Koegler, and Glen Meakem.

Bounce-Back Team: Courtney Hall, Lindsay Hale, Meredith Hibbetts.

College Prowler®
5001 Baum Blvd.
Suite 750
Pittsburgh, PA 15213

Phone: 1-800-290-2682
Fax: 1-800-772-4972
E-mail: info@collegeprowler.com
Web Site: www.collegeprowler.com

Welcome to College Prowler®

During the writing of College Prowler's guidebooks, we felt it was critical that our content was unbiased and unaffiliated with any college or university. We think it's important that our readers get honest information and a realistic impression of the student opinions on any campus—that's why if any aspect of a particular school is terrible, we (unlike a campus brochure) intend to publish it. While we do keep an eye out for the occasional extremist—the cheerleader or the cynic—we take pride in letting the students tell it like it is. We strive to create a book that's as representative as possible of each particular campus. Our books cover both the good and the bad, and whether the survey responses point to recurring trends or a variation in opinion, these sentiments are directly and proportionally expressed through our guides.

College Prowler guidebooks are in the hands of students throughout the entire process of their creation. Because you can't make student-written guides without the students, we have students at each campus who help write, randomly survey their peers, edit, layout, and perform accuracy checks on every book that we publish. From the very beginning, student writers gather the most up-to-date stats, facts, and inside information on their colleges. They fill each section with student quotes and summarize the findings in editorial reviews. In addition, each school receives a collection of letter grades (A through F) that reflect student opinion and help to represent contentment, prominence, or satisfaction for each of our 20 specific categories. Just as in grade school, the higher the mark the more content, more prominent, or more satisfied the students are with the particular category.

Once a book is written, additional students serve as editors and check for accuracy even more extensively. Our bounce-back team—a group of randomly selected students who have no involvement with the project—are asked to read over the material in order to help ensure that the book accurately expresses every aspect of the university and its students. This same process is applied to the 200-plus schools College Prowler currently covers. Each book is the result of endless student contributions, hundreds of pages of research and writing, and countless hours of hard work. All of this has led to the creation of a student information network that stretches across the nation to every school that we cover. It's no easy accomplishment, but it's the reason that our guides are such a great resource.

When reading our books and looking at our grades, keep in mind that every college is different and that the students who make up each school are not uniform—as a result, it is important to assess schools on a case-by-case basis. Because it's impossible to summarize an entire school with a single number or description, each book provides a dialogue, not a decision, that's made up of 20 different topics and hundreds of student quotes. In the end, we hope that this guide will serve as a valuable tool in your college selection process. Enjoy!

OMID GOHARI ◯ CHRISTINA KOSHZOW ◯ CHRIS MASON ◯ JOEY RAHIMI ◯ LUKE SKURMAN ◯
The College Prowler Team

Table of Contents

Introduction from the Author

HOOK 'EM HORNS! I could not have picked a better school to spend my four years at than the University of Texas at Austin. I don't think that there is anyone on the planet who hasn't heard of the largest and most recognized university in the lone-star state. You will be hard-pressed to find a school with students and alumni who are prouder of their alma mater. We at UT Austin exemplify the legendary Mack Brown's challenge: "Come Early, Stay Late, Be Loud, Wear Orange." No problem.

The University of Texas at Austin is a premiere public institution, not only in the state of Texas, but nationwide. The University is one of only three southwestern members of the Association of American Universities, which is composed of the 63 leading research institutions in North America. We are the largest university in the country, and we are proud of it. And why wouldn't we be? We have top-ranked academics, the 2002 *Sports Illustrated* #1-ranked athletics program among all Division I Schools, hundreds of student organizations, a beautiful campus with state-of-the-art facilities, all rolled up into one of the greatest cities known to modern culture: the live music capital of the U.S.—Austin, Texas.

There was never any question in my mind as to what school I was going to apply to. I wavered a little on deciding where I was going to go, but once I got here, I didn't regret my decision for a second. Coming to UT was, without a doubt, the best choice I have ever made in my life (all 18 years of it!). I have never had more fun while learning so much among so many amazing professors and students. At Texas, you are surrounded by some of the greatest people you will ever meet in your life. They say that the college years are the best years of your life. I say, "They're made so much better if you go to Texas."

However, some students at UT Austin don't feel the same way I do; the University, and the city of Austin, certainly has its drawbacks. Throughout the next 180 pages or so, hundreds of UT student opinions will be voiced and, be warned, not all students are as enthusiastic about their surroundings as I am.

To be certain, this guidebook probably will not be the deciding factor in whether or not you actually choose to attend school here. It will, however, serve as a director (or a tour guide, so to speak) of the inner-most workings of the University of Texas that you won't find in a school pamphlet or Web site. So, go on and read, learn, enjoy!

Erin Hall, Author
University of Texas at Austin

By the Numbers

General Information

University of Texas at Austin
1 University Station
Austin, Texas 78712

Control:
Public

Academic Calendar:
Semester

Religious Affiliation:
None

Founded:
1883

Web site:
www.utexas.edu

Main Phone:
(512) 471-3434

Admissions Phone:
(512) 475-7399

Student Body

**Full-Time
Undergraduates:**
33,888

**Part-Time
Undergraduates:**
3,489

**Total Male
Undergraduates:**
18,056

**Total Female
Undergraduates:**
19,321

Admissions

Overall Acceptance Rate:
51%

Regular Acceptance Rate:
51%

Total Applicants:
23,008

Total Acceptances:
11,788

Total Freshman Enrollment:
6,795

Yield (% of admitted students who actually enroll):
57%

Early Decision Available?
No

Early Action Available?
No

Regular Decision Deadline:
February 1

Regular Decision Notification:
Rolling Admissions, by April 1

Must-Reply-By Date:
May 1

Transfer Applications Received:
10,090

Transfer Applications Accepted:
2,366

Transfer Students Enrolled:
1,773

Transfer Application Acceptance Rate:
23%

Common Application Accepted?
Yes

Supplemental Forms?
Yes

Admissions E-mail:
askadmit@uts.cc.utexas.edu

Admissions Web Site:
http://www.utexas.edu/student/ admissions

Admissions Mailing Address:
UT Austin
Office of Admissions
P.O. Box 8058
Austin, TX 78713-8058

Admissions Street Address:
University of Texas at Austin
Office of Admissions
2400 Inner Campus Drive
Austin, TX 78712

University of Texas at Austin Houston Admissions Center
700 Fannin, Suite 110, Box 21
Houston, TX 77030
Phone: (713) 500-BEVO
E-mail: adhac@mail.utexas.edu

→

University of Texas at Austin Dallas Admissions Center
Exchange Park Mall
6333 Forest Park Road,
Suite 234A
Dallas, TX 75235
Phone: (214) 648-5204
Fax: (214) 648-5222
E-mail: addac@mail.utexas.edu

Graduate and International Admissions:
GIAC
UT Austin
2608 Whitis Ave.
Austin, TX 78712-1534
Phone: (512) 475-7390
Fax: (512) 475-7395

SAT I or ACT Required?
Yes, Either test. Your one highest composite score from any single test date is accepted.

First-Year Students Submitting SAT Scores:
95%

SAT I Range (25th – 75th Percentile):
1100-1340

SAT I Verbal Range (25th – 75th Percentile):
540-660

SAT I Math Range (25th – 75th Percentile):
570-680

Retention Rate:
92%

Top 10% of High School Class:
66%

Application Fee:
$50

Financial Information

In-State Tuition:
$5,735

Out-of-State Tuition:
$14,435

Room and Board:
$6,184

Books and Supplies for Class:
$762

Average Need-Based Financial Aid Package (including loans, work-study, grants, and other sources):
$9,250

Students Who Applied For Financial Aid:
71%

Students Who Received Aid:
53%

Financial Aid Forms Deadline:
None, Priority Date April

Financial Aid Phone:
(512) 475-6282

Financial Aid Fax:
(512) 475-6296

Financial Aid Office Location:
100 W. Dean Keeton St.

Student Services Building:
3rd Floor, Suite 3.200

Financial Aid Office Hours:
Monday-Friday 8 a.m.-5 p.m.,
Wednesday 9 a.m.-4:30 p.m.

Financial Aid E-mail:
finaid@www.utexas.edu

Financial Aid Web Site:
http://finaid.utexas.edu/

Did You Know?

The University of Texas tower is 307 feet tall, and with the main building, was built in the 1930s to house the University library.

The Tower's Knicker Carillon, the **largest carillon** in Texas, is made up of 56 bells.

The diameter of each **clock face on the Tower**, measured to the outside of the gold rim, is 14 feet, eight inches.

The Tower clock was **first set into motion in 1936**.

The Tower is constructed of **Bedford Indiana Limestone**.

Academics

The Lowdown On...
Academics

Degrees Awarded:
Bachelor
Master
Doctorate
First Professional

Most Popular Majors:
15% Social Sciences
14% Business, Management, Marketing
13% Communication, Journalism
10% Engineering
7% Biological, Biomedical Sciences

Undergraduate Schools:
Communication
Education
Engineering
Fine Arts
Liberal Arts
McCombs School of Business
Natural Sciences
Nursing
Pharmacy
Social Work

→

→

Full-Time Faculty:	**Average Course Load:**
2,467	14 hours

Faculty with Terminal Degree:
91%

Graduation Rate:
Four-Year: 39%
Five-Year: 67%
Six-Year: 74%

Student-to-Faculty Ratio:
19 to 1

Special Degree Options

Double majors—you can pretty much double major in anything you want, though some majors go together better than others. Honors Programs include Plan II, Dean's Scholars, Business Honors, as well as others. There are several graduate program options that can be completed simultaneously such as Law/MBA. Advanced Placement tests may be used for credit only. Scores accepted are 2, 3, 4, and 5.

"Top 10 Percent Rule"

Any Texas high school senior ranking in the top 10 percent of his or her high school class is granted automatic admission to any Texas state school, including the University of Texas at Austin. However, this does not guarantee you admission to the college of your choice.

Best Places to Study

UGL, PCL, Architecture Library, Starbucks, The Union

Sample Academic Clubs

Women in Computer Science, Undergraduate Philosophy Association, National Communication Association Student Club, Texas Advertising Group, University Finance Association, Liberal Arts Honors Student Council, Iota Sigma Chi-Women in Chemistry

Did You Know?

There are **more than 750 student organizations at UT**. And if you still can't find the one you want, you can form your own. You just need two friends, because with three people you can form your own club or student organization at UT. This is where some of the more interesting organizations here have come from, such as The Duncan Gilman Fan Club—Duncan Gilman is a student at UT.

In the Spring of 1974, one of the most infamous student organizations was formed—the **Association of Streaking Students (A.S.S.)**. Students really can create any kind of club they want.

There are more than **100 undergraduate degree programs**, 170 graduate degree programs, and more than 50 honors programs.

There are more than **350 study abroad opportunities** in 80 countries.

More than **400 patents** have been awarded to the University since its inception.

The fall 2003 incoming freshman class had the **highest academic qualifications in the University's history** and included the largest percentage of Hispanic students.

The largest college at the University, with **over 14,000 students, is the College of Liberal Arts**.

The University awards **11,000 degrees annually**, more than any other university.

Students Speak Out On...
Academics

"The teachers are very intelligent and very scholarly. Sometimes the intensity of their own research causes them to be more apathetic about the progress of their students."

Q "All of my professors at UT wrote the books used in our field (Communication Sciences and Disorders). They were very knowledgeable. The classes, for the most part, were also very interesting."

Q "For the most part, the teachers are awesome. Teachers keep my interest, even in the eight o'clock classes. Dr. Brandl in the business school is a great lecturer, so much so that he got a standing ovation the last day of class. Most of my classes are interesting, but there are some that make me feel like I'm back in high school again. The good ones open my eyes to new perspectives about the world around me."

Q "Most of my teachers are really good. Some put more effort into teaching than others, but all of them are well qualified. Some of my classes are pretty interesting—it can depend a lot on who the professor is and how the material is covered. On the other hand, some classes will be boring no matter what, just because they cover boring material."

Q "The teachers I've had so far are pretty good; they are very knowledgeable of the topics they teach, and they are willing to take the time to get to know you as long as you take the initiative to introduce yourself."

Q "If you are a communication studies major, Vangelisti, Knapp and Daly are the professors to take for any classes that they are teaching. They are all **amazing and fun lecturers who teach entertaining classes**. Some of their classes are Interpersonal Communication Theory, Lying and Deception, Nonverbal Communication, Communication and Personal Relationships, and Family Communication."

Q "A side note on the Business Foundations Certificate Program—you don't actually have to finish the program to put it on your resume. All you would get for finishing the program is a certificate, which no one in a job interview is going to ask to see. If you really want the certificate to hang in your office someday, then by all means, finish the program. However, if you just want to take just some of the courses and put it on your resume as 'Business Foundations Minor or Concentration' **you can do that whether you get the certificate or not**."

Q "I have had some amazing teachers and TAs at UT. Some are horrible, but their names get out and you usually don't take a class with them unless you have to. If at all possible, **take RTF [Radio-Television-Film] 314 with Professor Frick**. The class is amazing, and everyone loves her. Also, if you are an RTF major, be sure and take Charles Ramirez-Berg for as many classes as possible. Even if the class does not sound interesting to you at all, take it just to have him as your professor. This man is absolutely amazing, and he's so kind and thoroughly enjoyable to listen to. He is one of Robert Rodriguez's mentors. When I was in one of Charles's classes, Robert Rodriguez came to speak to us. He showed us the film he did for Charles's class when he was a student called "Bedhead." The class was a very cool experience. Charles is just a really amazing man, and he's one of my favorite teachers at UT."

Q "**Beware of TAs who don't speak the language**! Change your TA section the first week if you can't understand them or if your grade depends on them. I'm in Plan II, so I have had several smaller classes (15 to 20 students) since the beginning, which is phenomenal, except that you can't skip. Beginning foreign language classes are an enormous undertaking; don't take one the fall of your freshman year because it won't go well. Foreign language classes should not be in the morning! Professor Woods for E603A or B (a Plan II literature class) is amazing! I don't recommend Bio 211 and 212 in one semester, even though you can take them concurrently—it's too much information at once. I don't recommend getting too socially involved with your major—barbecues and such are fine, parties on Friday nights are not okay."

Q "**Some teachers are cool, others I'd like to punch in the face**. It's basically the same anywhere you go. Oh, and don't take any classes before 11:00 a.m."

Q "Unfortunately, the teaching atmosphere at UT, at least within the natural sciences department, is **too focused on research rather than teaching ability**. In my experience, many professors clearly demonstrate that they do not enjoy being in the classroom, and I feel it is reflected in the students' understanding of the material. Don't get me wrong, there have been many professors that absolutely amaze me in how effectively they can teach. These few professors make up for a lot of what is lacking in the University's teaching quality."

Q "Professors are varied. For many of the lower division courses, (freshman, sophomore), **more than one professor teaches the course**, and invariably, one will be better than the others. Ask someone who has already taken the course which professor they like. Also, CIS (Course Instructor Surveys) results, or *www.pickaprof.com* can help. In general, the professors are very knowledgeable and organized."

The College Prowler Take On...
Academics

The University of Texas is one of the top public universities in the country and is consistently ranked in the top 50 public universities in the country. We have top-ranked programs in accounting, engineering, and communication studies, just to name a few. The professors at UT run the gamut—some are great and genuinely care about their students, and some have written the textbooks that are used in their classes and aren't as interested in students' input. Others are only teaching so that they can stay at Texas to further their research. Most likely in your career here at Texas, you will have at least one of each different kind of teacher, but the majority of our professors here are wonderful and will give you a great experience. Some classes at UT are rather large, over 100 people, but that doesn't make them inferior, nor does it preclude learning. Some of the best classes that I have taken here at UT have been huge and over 100 people. In these large classes, there are generally several TAs that you can utilize, and you should always take advantage of a professor's office hours. This can help to make the large lecture class seem smaller. Depending on your major, and especially once you get into upper division classes, there are generally smaller classes with more individual attention.

There are two classes at UT that everyone should take as electives while they are a student: EDP 367 Human Sexuality and CMS 315M Interpersonal Communication Theory. These are two of the most interesting and fun classes that the majority of students here eventually wind up taking. While neither are blow-off classes, they both teach you a lot and are enjoyable to study for.

B

The College Prowler® Grade on
Academics: B

A high Academics grade generally indicates that professors are knowledgeable, accessible, and genuinely interested in their students' welfare. Other determining factors include class size, how well professors communicate, and whether or not classes are engaging.

Local Atmosphere

The Lowdown On...
Local Atmosphere

Region:
Southwest

City, State:
Austin, Texas

Setting:
Medium-sized city

Distance from Houston:
2 hours, 30 minutes

Distance from Dallas:
3 hours

Points of Interest:
Barton Creek Greenbelt
The Bats
Governor's Mansion
Mount Bonnell
South Congress
Texas History Museum
Texas State Capital Building
Zilker Park

→

Closest Shopping Malls:

Arboretum

10000 Research Blvd.

(512) 338-4437

Take Mopac North to 183 North and exit 183 immediately at the Loop 360/Capital of Texas Highway/Great Hills Trail Exit. Then, either turn left onto 360 and follow it until you can turn right off of 360 into the Arboretum (its not far), or go straight through the light at 360 to the next light which is Great Hills Trail, turn left at the light, go under the overpass, and the Arboretum will be on either side of you.

Barton Creek Square Mall

2901 S. Capital of Texas Hwy.

(512) 327-7041

Take Mopac South, exit 360N, then take the immediate right into the mall outer circle, get in left lane and turn into mall.

Highland Mall

6001 Airport Blvd.

(512) 454-9656

Take I-35 North, keep Right at the fork in the Ramp at Airport Blvd. Turn left on Airport Blvd., and follow it around until you see the mall.

Prime Outlets At San Marcos

3939 S. I H 35 # 300

(512) 396-2200

Take I-35 South to San Marcos, exit number 200, and you will see the outlet mall stores on your left.

Fun Austin Stores:

Any Occasion
504 W. 24th St. # D
(512) 478-2255
Jewelry, sorority store—this store is great and has fun stuff for Greeks and just for gifts.

Blackmail 1202
1202 S. Congress Ave.
(512) 326-7670
Clothes—some vintage, some new, all black/

Bookpeople Book Store
603 N. Lamar Blvd.
(512) 472-5050
Books—great bookstore with fabulous selection/

Breed and Co. Hardware-Houseware
718 W. 29th St.
(512) 474-6679
Hardware, gifts—fun store to walk around in, home repair items and paint to stemware and candles/

By George
2346 Guadalupe St.
(512) 472-2731
Clothes and shoes—very nice clothes and shoes, always cute stuff and great brands.

(Fun Austin Stores, continued)

The Cadeau
2316 Guadalupe St.
(512) 477-7276
Clothes, gifts, jewelry, cards—
nice, upscale.

Crofts Original
1714 S. Congress Ave.
(512) 472-4028
Gifts, clothes—variety of fun
stuff to choose from/

Fetish
1112 N. Lamar Blvd.
(512) 457-1007
Shoes, clothes—fabulous shoe
selection, great designers.

Giada
704 W. 6th St.
(512) 457-8881
Boutique, fun clothes/

Groopie
807 W. 12th St.
(512) 472-1212
Gifts—fun stuff to check out,
usually trendy new items/

Julian Gold
1214 W. 6th St.
(512) 473-2493
Upscale department store/

Nordstrom Barton
(Barton Creek Square Mall)
2901 S. Capital of Texas Hwy.
(512) 691-3500
Upscale department store—
great makeup counters
and shoes/

Red Wing Shoe Store
3005 S. Lamar Blvd. #115
(512) 443-3766
Boots—for the pledging
fraternity boy.

Saks 5th Ave
9722 Great Hills Trail
(Arboretum)
(512) 231-3700
Upscale department store/

Shiki
3407 Guadalupe St. # H
(512) 371-7767
Nice, fun clothes.

Tinseltown South
5501 S I H 35
(512) 326-3800
Take I-35 South, exit 230A,
turn left on Stassney, then
take feeder road North to
Tinseltown South/

Therapy
1113 S. Congress Ave.
(512) 326-2331
Cool clothes, a very in place to
shop.

Toy Joy
2900 Guadalupe St.
(512) 320-0090
Toys—this is a fun store to go
into and revert to childhood.

Urban Outfitters
2406 Guadalupe St.
(512) 472-1621
Clothes, gifts, home décor,
shoes—funky, trendy, different.

Ven Shoe Salon
3801 N. Capital of Texas Hwy.
Suite #G
(512) 306-8200
Shoes—fun shoes, in the same
shopping center as Vylette.

Vylette
3801 N. Capital of Texas Hwy.
(512) 347-7878
Clothes—very hip place to
shop, great stuff.

Closest
Movie Theatres:

Alamo Drafthouse
Downtown
409 Colorado St.
(512) 476-1320
Take Guadalupe South, left on
5th, right on Colorado/

Dobie Theatre
2021 Guadalupe St.
(512) 472-3456
Take Guadalupe South, turn
left on 21st St.

Regal Metropolitan Stadium 14
901 Little Texas Ln.
(512) 447-0101
Take I-35 South Exit 230 A,
turn right on Little Texas Lane/

Major Sports Teams:

Austin Ice Bats
(Hockey)

Round Rock Express
(Minor League Baseball)

Austin Wrangler
(Arena Football)

Texas Longhorns

Did You Know?

The films *The Rookie, The Faculty, The Life of David Gale, Spy Kids, The New Guy, The Alamo, Cheer Up, Dazed and Confused, Slacker, Texas Chainsaw Massacre: The New Generation, Texas Chainsaw Massacre* (2003), *Varsity Blues, Miss Congeniality, Lone Star State of Mind,* and *The Newton Boys* are just **some of the recent films that have been made in Austin**.

In 2003, Austin was ranked 4th on *Travel and Leisure's* poll of Best Loved Cities, 1st on the *Forbes* list of **Best Cities for Singles,** and 3rd on *Hispanic Magazine's* Best Cities for Hispanics.

In 2002, *Money* magazine rated Austin one of the **Top 10 Best Places to Live**, and *USA Today* said that Austin was 4th in Best Cultural Attractions, 5th in Best Nightlife, 5th Friendliest City in the Country, 3rd Best City in the Spring, and 3rd overall in Best-Looking People.

Famous People From Austin:

Lance Armstrong (cyclist)

Asleep at the Wheel (band)

Stone Cold Steve Austin (wrestler)

Marcia Ball (musician)

Ray Bensen (musician)

Sandra Bullock (actress)

Michael Dell (computers)

The Fabulous Thunderbirds (band)

Fastball (band)

Pat Green (musician)

O. Henry (writer)

Tobe Hooper (director)

Janis Joplin (musician)

Richard Linklater (director)

Matthew McConaughey (actor)

Benjamin McKenzie (actor)

Willie Nelson (musician)

Robert Rodriguez (director)

Spoon (band)

Bob Schneider (musician)

Quentin Tarantino (actor/director)

Stevie Ray Vaughn (musician)

Django Walker (musician)

Jerry Jeff Walker (musician)

→

5 Fun Facts about Austin:

- Janis Joplin was voted the Ugliest Man on Campus.

- Matthew McConaughey was arrested for playing the bongos naked in his house in Tarrytown just west of the University.

- The best snow cone stand in Austin is located on Lamar Boulevard, right before Barton Springs when you are driving south. It is called Sno Beach. You have to try their snow cones with cream; they are delicious!

- Every spring, Austin celebrates Eeyore's Birthday Party. It was started in 1963 by a group of UT frat guys and was invitation-only. It has grown larger every year, and it's now a fundraiser benefiting local charities. You will definitely find all kinds of people at Eeyore's Birthday, from students, to hippies, to ex-students bringing their kids to experience what they experienced 40 years ago.

- We have our own local celebrity: Leslie. He does have a last name, it is Cochran, but he is known to everyone simply as Leslie. He is a transient transvestite who walks around Austin generally wearing a thong and tutu and tank top. He has recently gotten breast implants. He has a bike with a cardboard box house built up around it with various sentiments written on it, many blasting the Austin police force.

Other Things to Do:

Golf

Pease Park Disc Golf
1100 Kingsburgh St.
(512) 499-6700

Zilker Park Disc Golf
2201 Barton Springs Rd.
(512) 482-8076

Peter Pan Mini Golf
1207 Barton Springs Rd.
(512) 472-1033

Putt Putt Golf and Games
6700 Burnet Rd.
(512) 454-8644

Zoo

Austin Zoo
10807 Rawhide Trl.
(512) 288-1490

Outdoor Activities

Boat Rentals
http://www.austin360.com

Hamilton Pool
24300 Hamilton Pool Rd.
(512) 264-2740

Barton Springs Pool
2201 Barton Springs Rd.
(512) 476-9044

Deep Eddy Pool
401 Deep Eddy Ave.
(512) 472-8546

Sports Complexes:

Round Rock Express
3400 E Palm Valley Blvd.
(512) 671-8376

Dell Diamond
3400 E. Palm Valley Blvd.
(512) 255-2255

(Sports Complexes, continued)

Round Rock Rollar Rink
15501 Ranch Road 620 N.
(512) 218-0103

Laser Quest
523 Highland Mall Blvd.
(512) 459-5400

Blazer Tag
1701 W. Ben White Blvd.
(512) 462-0202

Arts, Music, and Theatre

Dougherty Arts Center
1110 Barton Springs Rd.
(512) 397-1468

State Theater
713 Congress Ave.
(512) 472-5143

Paramount Theatre for
Performing Arts
713 Congress Ave.
(512) 472-5470

Zachary Scott Theatre
1510 Toomey Rd.
(512) 476-0594

Bass Concert Hall
2400 E. Campus Dr.
(512) 471-5401

Bowling

Union Underground Bowling
24th & Guadalupe
(512) 475-6670

Highland Lanes Bowling
8909 Burnet Rd.
(512) 458-1215

AMF Showplace Lanes
9504 North IH 35
(512) 834-7733

(Other Things to Do, continued):

Yoga, Exercise

Yoga Yoga
2167 W. Anderson Ln.
(512) 380-9800

Rolling Hills Yoga
2520 Longview St. # 412
(512) 288-7238

UT Informal Classes
www.informalclasses.org

Water Adventure

There are more than 30 miles of running trails in Austin-including Shoal Creek, Barton Creek, Town Lake and more.

Schlitterbahn-New Braunfels
305 W. Austin St.
(830) 625-2351
Tubing in New Braunfels on the Guadalupe, Gruene and San Marcos Rivers.

Local Slang:

Congress - A main street downtown that runs into the Capital.

South Congress - the part of Congress Avenue where there are many cool shops that trendy people like to frequent.

First Thursday - on S. Congress Avenue on the first Thursday of every month there is an open house of sorts where all of the stores are open late and people can walk around and eat and drink and shop and listen to music. It is very popular.

The Drag - Guadalupe Street while it is in front of the University, there are lots of shops and restaurants that are very popular with students and with tourists visiting UT.

Co-op - The store on the Drag that sells UT memorabilia and books for UT classes.

Leslie - A local celebrity—Austin's very famous transvestite.

City Web Sites

www.austin.citysearch.com

www.austin-chamber.org

www.ci.austin.tx.us

www.austin360.com

Students Speak Out On...
Local Atmosphere

{ **"Austin is a laid-back place with lots of different things to do. There are other schools here, but they don't matter. There are a million things to visit in and around Austin."**

Q "Austin is pretty friendly. West Austin has nicer neighborhoods. **Don't go to East Austin, it's dangerous**. South Austin is sometimes referred to as Bubba-Land by older Austinites. While it's openly liberal, there are conservative people if you know where to look. It is a very political city, as there is always some issue."

Q "Austin is such a free place. There is so much to do and see here, and I think that is why people choose this university over others. There aren't one or two dominant types of people; instead **there are many types, and the area will cater to almost any kind of person**. There are a few other colleges in this city, yet there is almost no rivalry because most people here have taken classes at these other colleges . . . and they're small anyway. The best places to visit are all outdoors. Austin has a large environmental group, and thus many parks and outdoors recreational facilities are available. Make sure to also go to at least one outdoor concert or else you have not really experienced Austin."

Q "**Austin is a really laid-black town** with stuff for everyone. There's always something going on every night of the week if you want it. In the spring, definitely go visit the capital grounds and sit out there to do homework."

Q "It's always charged here in Austin. There's always something to do, and if you're not careful you could be sucked into spreading yourself too thin. The thing about Austin is that it is so great that **you can enjoy both ends of the spectrum**. You can go to a crazy concert in Zilker Park, or the quiet, cozy surroundings of Spiderhouse Coffeehouse."

Q "**The atmosphere changes with the seasons**, I suppose. The summer is as laid-back as can be, and the fall seems to be full of stress for most. The spring is a little more laid-back. I assume it is because people become settled and have less on their minds. There are other universities around, the most noticeable being the community college."

Q "**Stay away from The Boys' Cellar**, and pretty much any bar on 4th street."

Q "Austin is an amazing and liberal city. I grew up in Denver, Colorado, a very liberal environment in itself, but never before did I imagine a place where any type of person can fit in. **Although the city itself is growing rapidly, I still feel it maintains its small-town feel**. There is nothing that I would stay away from, and I advise visiting as many local and unique places as possible."

Q "There are a couple of other universities in town, but UT is so big that you really don't have to look beyond campus. Austin is so diverse, so make sure you do venture away from campus every once in a while. **Check out Lake Travis and the west side of town** . . . stay west of I-35! It's scary on the East Side!"

Q "There are **too many protests and liberals** for me."

The College Prowler Take On...
Local Atmosphere

You really couldn't ask for a much better college town than Austin, Texas, the Live Music Capital of the World. There is so much to do in Austin and definitely something for everyone—bars, museums, parks, lakes, running trails, kayaking, shopping, coffee houses, outdoor music venues, smoky blues clubs, naked swimming at Hippie Hollow. We even have our own little beach in central Texas—Volente Waterpark Beach.

Austin is a city with a small-town feel, and that is what most people love about it. When you live near UT, you are two minutes from downtown. People around here are walking everywhere, there is a lot of biking, and the people couldn't be friendlier. Everyone loves the laid-back atmosphere of Austin, and the fact that anything goes. On any day of the week, you can sit around outside people watching for hours and keep yourself entertained. The fun thing about Austin is that if you want to just be lazy and relax by the lake or at the park, you can do that. But if you want to be active, there are tons of places to run, bike, swim, hike, kayak, climb, or pretty much anything you can imagine. The 50,000 students of the University of Texas include so many different kinds of people with so many different kinds of interests that they blend right in to the laid-back, but always fun town that is Austin.

A+

The College Prowler® Grade on
Local
Atmosphere: A+

A high Local Atmosphere grade indicates that the area surrounding campus is safe and scenic. Other factors include nearby attractions, proximity to other schools, and the town's attitude toward students.

Safety & Security

The Lowdown On...
Safety & Security

Number of UT Police:
67

UT Police Phone:
(512) 471-4441

Safety Services:
RAD
SURE Walk
70 Call-boxes
Property and Personal
Safety Program
Tactical Communication
Program to reduce
Confrontations

(Safety Services, continued)
Self-defense classes
Designated Driver Program
(512) 471-5200
E-Bus
Silent Witness
K-9 Unit
Police Escort Van
Bicycle Registration

Health Services:
Birth Control Available at
University Health Center
for $10

Health Center Office Hours:
Monday-Friday
8:30 a.m.-5 p.m.

Health Center Web site:
www.utexas.edu/student/ health

24-Hour Nurse Advice Line:
(512) 475-NURSE

Appointments:
(512) 471-4955

Did You Know?

You can become a **Sexual Health Peer Advisor or an Alcohol and Drug Education Peer Advisor** at the University Health Services and receive class credit, as well as volunteer your time and learn valuable information.

Students Speak Out On...
Safety & Security

"Security doesn't seem to be a problem around campus since there always seems to be enough people around to make you feel safe."

Q "Security is great, and **I feel really safe**."

Q "**The only scary place on campus is the libraries**, because they are too quiet and the stacks are so tall that no one would ever know if you got lost in there or something. That is why I never go to the libraries, especially the PCL."

Q "**Campus is safe**. Take it from me, I'm a girl who weighs 110 pounds!"

Q "I am very impressed with how safe I always feel on such a large campus. There has **never been a moment where I felt I needed to be extra cautious**."

Q "The security call-boxes seem far apart from each other, but **campus police has pretty high visibility on campus**. Don't be too afraid of the homeless people; they are part of the Austin scene."

Q "Austin is known for its safety. I cannot really answer what security is like on campus since there is no need for it really. However, **there are call-boxes placed sporadically throughout the campus**, and SURE Walk is available for people walking across campus and the surrounding areas at night."

Q "Being a male, **I feel safe whenever I'm on campus**."

Q "Security is decent, but **Guadalupe is scary at night**. I try to walk with a boy or a group of girls after dark."

Q "Security on campus is very impressive with phone booths lit up all over campus. **Police constantly patrol here**, and I feel surprisingly safe for having grown up in a small town and moving to the city."

Q "**Safety and security is pretty high**. I always feel safe, although I know some females feel a little unsafe walking through campus at night."

Q "I'm a girl, and I used to walk across campus to Gregory Gym at night. **Campus was well lit**, and there were always people there at night. I've felt safe, but I always carry mace just in case."

The College Prowler Take On...
Safety & Security

Overall, students feel safe on campus. The UT campus is well lit, there are generally at least some people on campus at all times, and programs such as SURE Walk (which offers a walk late at night home from the libraries on campus), and UTPD Escort Service, both contributing to better feelings of security to students. There are a few guys that do not feel safe walking on campus alone, and many girls feel safe walking alone, as well. However, it is a good policy to walk with others rather than alone. Campus police are usually seen on campus, and there are blue-light phones that will notify police of your location on campus if there is ever an emergency. While most girls feel safe walking on the actual campus alone at night, the areas surrounding campus are a different story. In the West Campus area there are definitely dangers. There have been various "West Campus Rapists." Walking alone in West Campus at night is unsafe behavior. However, if you take general precautions, Austin and the campus area are safe.

Just be smart and don't take unnecessary risks. Austin is not a high crime city—we're not living in inner-city Houston or Los Angeles or New York. Austin is a much quieter town crime-wise, not to say things don't happen. But for the most part, if you are aware of your surroundings, and especially if you are on campus, safety and security are a non-issue.

B+

The College Prowler® Grade on

Safety & Security: B+

A high grade in Safety & Security means that students generally feel safe, campus police are visible, blue-light phones and escort services are readily available, and safety precautions are not overly necessary.

Computers

The Lowdown On...
Computers

High-Speed Network?
Yes

Wireless Network?
Yes

Number of Labs:
59

Number of Computers:
400

24-Hour Labs
No

Operating Systems:
PC, MAC, Linux

Discounted Software

Windows XP Professional Upgrade $6.00, Office XP Professional $15.00, Office 2000 Professional $15.00, Front Page 2002 $6.00, Publisher 2002 $10.00, Adobe Photoshop $265.00, Pagemaker $254.00, Premiere 7 $211.00, Acrobat 6.0 $88.00, Final Cut Pro $399.00, Apple Works $45.00, Flash MX 04 $95.00, Dreamweaver MX 04 $42.00, Quicken 2003 Deluxe $58.00

Charge to Print?

Yes, printed sheets can be charged on your Bevo Bucks card.

Did You Know?

UT's Web site, *www.utexas.edu*, has been known to **receive more than 680,000 hits per day**.

Students Speak Out On...
Computers

> **"Computer labs can get crowded at certain times of the day and during finals and midterms. While it's not imperative that one has his or her own computer, it would be a great idea for convenience."**

Q "The computer network is excellent. Computer labs have many people in them at certain times, but you can always find a computer. I would recommend bringing your own computer, but **you can definitely get by without one**. If you are a member of the business school, laptops are available for checkout at no charge."

Q "I suppose the network reliability depends on where you are. **The network keeps getting better and better**. UT has added wireless access points in many places, and also provided more wired connections on campus. The labs are crowded at certain times, but you can almost always find one open. Bringing your own computer is more convenient to finish those procrastination projects."

Q "The computer network is extremely fast. **The labs in the business school have their peak hours, but you can usually find an open computer**. Bring your own computer because you might not always want to make the trek to school. Preferably bring your laptop so you can utilize the new wireless Internet service on campus."

Q "There are many computer labs on campus, but many people only go to the crowded, popular ones. With a little hunting, you can find many labs that people don't go to. **Having your own home computer is a must** because so many professors e-mail information daily."

Q "In this age of technological advances, I feel that it has become necessary to have a computer of your own. This is not to say that you won't be using computers on campus, for **you will actually use the labs quite often**. But it is important to stay constant on new word processing programs, as well as other new educational tools."

Q "Bring a computer! It's possible to survive without your own, but **it saves you a lot of walking**. Most computer labs are easily accessible on campus, and you can still print stuff out for a fee. My printer was out for a month, and I lived in the UGL lab."

Q "I would bring my own computer just for the convenience of doing work at home. **The labs are very good**. There are times where they can be crowded, but there are several available all over campus."

Q "In order to use computers on campus you have to **remember your IF account number and password that they give you at orientation**. So, be sure to save that little piece of paper that you write it down on, because whenever you get back to school and want to use a computer on campus, you will need it. Also, the people at the labs aren't supposed to look it up for you, or if they are, they don't like to help you out. I kept my little piece of paper with that written on in it in my purse for probably two years and then took it out because I never needed it. Of course, as soon as I did that, I needed it and couldn't find it. So, my advice is to save that or memorize the number and your password."

Q "I was fortunate enough to always have my own computer during college, and **I used my friends' printers when I needed to**."

The College Prowler Take On...
Computers

Though the University of Texas is well equipped with lots of computer labs and many computers (both PCs and Macs), the number of students far outnumbers the number of computers. It really is best to bring your own computer if you are able to do so. But if you are not, there is usually a computer available in one of the many labs on campus. Some of the largest labs are located in FAC 212 with 173 computers, the CBA with 245, and the PCL with 71 computers. The overall student consensus is that bringing your own computer is a great idea, and it is even better if you can bring a laptop. However, one thing you have to think about is that one of the great things about dorms is the networks and the availability of tons of music to download (not that I would ever "steal" or condone "stealing music"). If you have a laptop, you only have so much storage space, and this is where a desktop comes in handy. However, with CD burners, tons of storage space is really unnecessary.

There is a wireless network available in most buildings on campus, so if you have a laptop you can be connected to the Internet even while you are in class. If you are in the business school, they will allow you to check out laptops and other equipment such as projectors, using your student ID. The Campus Computer Store will allow students to purchase many types of software at very discounted prices, and this is very well worth checking out. The store is located behind Gregory Gym.

The College Prowler® Grade on

Computers: B-

A high grade in Computers designates that computer labs are available, the computer network is easily accessible, and the campus' computing technology is up-to-date.

Facilities

The Lowdown On...
Facilities

Student Center:
Yes, the Texas Union

Athletic Center:
Anna Hiss Gym, Bellmont Hall, Clark Field, Gregory Gym, Jamail Texas Swimming Center, Penick-Allison Tennis Center, PRC Commons Rec Center (PRC), Recreational Sports Center (the Rec), Whitaker Fields, Whitaker Tennis

Campus Size:
350 acres

Libraries:
Architecture and Planning Library: Monday-Thursday 9 a.m.-10 p.m., Friday 9 a.m.-5 p.m., Saturday 12-6 p.m., Sunday 3-10 p.m.

Benson Latin American Collection: Monday-Friday 9 a.m.-6 p.m., Saturdays 1-5 p.m., Sundays 2-10 p.m.

Center for American History: Monday-Saturday 9 a.m.-5 p.m.

→

Classics Library:
Monday-Friday 8 a.m.-5 p.m.

Fine Arts Library:
Monday-Thursday 8 a.m.-
10 p.m., Friday 8 a.m.-5 p.m.
Saturday 1 p.m.-5 p.m.,
Sunday 1 p.m.-10 p.m.

Harry Ransom Center:
Monday-Friday 9 a.m.-5 p.m.,
Saturday 9 a.m.-12 p.m.

Kuehne Physics-Math-
Astronomy Library:
Monday-Thursday 8 a.m.-
10 p.m., Friday 8 a.m.-5 p.m.,
Saturday 1-5 p.m., Sunday
2-10 p.m.

Life Science Library:
Monday-Thursday 8 a.m.-
10 p.m., Friday 8 a.m.-6 p.m.,
Saturday 1 p.m.-5 p.m.,
Sunday 12-10:00 p.m.

Mallet Chemistry Library:
Monday-Thursday 8 a.m.-
10 p.m., Friday 8 a.m.-7 p.m.,
Saturday 1-5 p.m., Sunday
1-10 p.m.

McKinney Engineering Library:
Monday-Thursday, 8 a.m.-
10 p.m., Friday, 8 a.m.-5 p.m.,
Saturday 1-5 p.m., Sunday
2-10 p.m.

Perry Castaneda Library (PCL,
main library):
Monday-Friday 7 a.m.-2 a.m.,
Saturday 9 a.m.-12 a.m.,
Sunday 12 p.m.-2 a.m.

Tarlton Law Library:
Monday-Thursday 7:30 a.m.-
12 a.m., Friday 7:30 a.m.-
6 p.m., Saturday 10 a.m.-
7p.m., Sunday 10 a.m.-12 a.m.

Undergraduate Library (UGL):
Monday-Thursday 24 hours,
Friday closes at 10:00 p.m.,
Saturday 9 a.m.-10:00 p.m.,
Sunday opens at 12:00 p.m.

Walter Geology Library:
Monday-Thursday 8 a.m.-
10 p.m., Friday 8 a.m.-6 p.m.,
Saturday 1-5 p.m., Sunday
2-10 p.m.

Popular Places to Chill:

South Mall

The Tower Steps

The West Mall

Favorite Things to Do:

Bowling at the Union

Drink at the Cactus Café

Eat at the Union

Movies at Dobie Theatre

Sit on the Tower steps or
South Mall

Work out at Gregory or
the Rec

What Is There to Do On Campus?
Go to the gym, movies at the Union or Dobie, (off-campus private dorm with a small mall on the base level), bowling at the Union Underground, Dobie Mall, Cactus Café/Bar, shopping on the Drag, or eat at the Union or other campus restaurants.

Movie Theatre on Campus?
Yes, Dobie and Union

Bowling on Campus?
Yes, Union Underground

Bar on Campus?
Yes, Cactus Café

Coffeehouse on Campus?
Yes, in the Union or Starbucks, Peet's, Mojo's, or Metro

Did You Know?

UT's **first athletic field** was named for James Clark. He was not only the University librarian, but the registrar, and the groundskeeper.

Most of the buildings on campus are built in the **Spanish Renaissance architectural style**.

Paul Philipe Cret was supervising architect for the UT campus and designed 19 buildings including the main building and the Tower.

The University of Texas recently acquired the Watergate papers and will house the **archives of Woodward and Bernstein in the Harry Ransom Center**. Under terms of an agreement, the bulk of the archives were made available for public examination in March 2004.

Students Speak Out On...
Facilities

> **"They're numerous, and for the most part clean. Gregory is great. The Union is a great place to hang out and people watch."**

Q "I think the facilities are good, some are older, but for the most part, they are good. The business school is amazing, and the communications building has some newly renovated rooms that are nice, even if **the outside looks like an eyesore**. The communications building is an unattractive brown because it was originally painted with a special paint that, when oxidized, would turn to a perfect burnt orange. However, it unfortunately turned maroon (like the Aggie color), and was immediately painted over with the brown color it is today."

Q "The facilities are nice for the most part. **A few buildings don't have very good lecture halls**. All business school classes are nice and have great technological systems, including wireless Internet access in class."

Q "The facilities are constantly improving. **The engineering buildings are probably the oldest and most rundown,** but will most likely be the last to receive renovations. (They often depend on donations, and a larger portion of the engineering program consists of international students or people not as involved with their college). The business school facilities are among the best in the nation, and much of the University is following those standards. The athletic facilities can compare to most anywhere. The restricted athletic facilities (athletic program facilities) are unmatched."

Q "Gregory Gym is cool, the **Rec Center is the best place to work out because it's not as crowded**."

Q "The facilities are extremely nice on campus. With so many students, **there is more money for these buildings** and the University is one of the nicest I have ever seen."

Q "The Texas Union is an interesting place on campus. Since so much is going on around campus at any one time, it's hard to figure out what's going on in advance. Usually you can find something random in the Union, **from an MC battle, to impromptu classical piano**, to a lunar festival. Films are screened on weeknights for free. Belly dancing one night, swing dancing the next—it's great."

Q "All of buildings (athletic center, computer labs, and student center) are nice and relatively new. There are older classrooms and buildings on campus; but **nothing is ever dirty or smells funny**. It's all nice."

Q "Everything is really nice. **Gregory Gym is my home away from home**—it has so many machines, an indoor track, sport courts, and lots of aerobic programs."

Q "The facilities on campus are very nice. **The gym facilities are clean and contain the latest equipment**. The computer labs carry the most recent technology. Lots of people speak badly about the Health Center, but my one experience was great and quick."

Q "I think that the facilities are average. They are definitely nice enough to get the job done. There are some newer buildings that are really nice. **The athletic and recreational facilities are huge and well maintained**."

Q "One of the greatest resources is the Undergraduate Writing Center in the UGL. If you take a paper to them, they will check it for grammatical mistakes and meet with you on ways to improve your writing, which is always helpful. It also helps you not to procrastinate on papers. The Health Center is scary at best. Never go to a gynecologist at the Health Center, they will tell you that you are pregnant no matter what. Any doctor in the Health Center's first question is always, 'Are you pregnant?' No matter your response, you are guilty until proven innocent. I'm sure they ask the boys if they are pregnant, as well! Nothing is more frustrating than going into the Health Center with a sinus infection and having them treat you like a harlot. **You leave with a guilty conscience and condoms**, even if you are a virgin."

Q "The athletic center is awesome. Now that I'm a new graduate in Austin, **I really miss being able to use Gregory**."

Q "The facilities are satisfactory, but the better ones are usually in the business or computer science buildings. The plus to this is that you can use them even if your major is not one of those, but most people don't know that. Athletics are really impressive here. **We have a wonderful swim center and many great gyms**."

Q "The Health Center on campus is very helpful. The Ford Career Center in the business school, if utilized, **will help you with your future career decisions and questions**."

The College Prowler Take On...
Facilities

The University of Texas has great facilities that should definitely be utilized while you are here. We have great equipment in our gym and Rec Center: machines, weights, a pool, volleyball courts, racquetball courts, an indoor track, and a climbing wall. A few blocks away from the University proper are the intramural fields, located at Guadalupe and 51st Streets, where students can play various sports (soccer, football, Frisbee). The Texas Union is a great place to study, relax, grab a bite to eat, watch TV, or make copies. The second floor chairs are a comfortable place to either hang out or take a quick nap.

The University of Texas has more than a dozen libraries, and permanent exhibits include the Gutenberg Bible and the world's first photograph. The Benson is the largest collection of Latin American books in North America and they can be acessed by any UTA student. There is an Undergraduate Writing Center located on campus in the UGL where you can get help editing your papers and work on your writing skills free of charge. There are career centers within every college, as well as the large career center in Jester. Also in Jester is the Jester Learning Center where you can receive walk-in tutoring in many subjects.

The College Prowler® Grade on

Facilities: A

A high Facilities grade indicates that the campus is aesthetically pleasing and well-maintained; facilities are state-of-the-art, and libraries are exceptional. Other determining factors include the quality of both athletic and student centers and an abundance of things to do on campus.

Campus Dining

The Lowdown On...
Campus Dining

Freshman Meal Plan Requirement?
Yes, if living on campus

Meal Plan Average Cost:
Room cost includes $1200 Dining Dollars and $300 Bevo Bucks

Places to Grab a Bite with Your Meal Plan:
Students receive 10 percent off when they use Bevo Bucks at any of these dining hall locations that accept them.

40 Acres Bakery
Food: cookies, pastries, Starbucks coffee
Location: Jester

Favorite Dish: Starbucks' caramel macchiato, monster chocolate chip cookies

Hours: Monday-Friday 7 a.m.-2 p.m.

Dining Dollars and Bevo Bucks

Bene Pizza

Food: pizza

Location: Texas Union

Favorite Dish: smoked chicken and gouda pizza

Hours: Monday-Thursday 10:30 a.m.-6:30 p.m., Friday 10:30 a.m.-5:30 p.m., Saturday and Sunday closed

The Bistro

Food: sandwiches, salads

Location: Texas Union

Favorite Dish: turkey sandwich

Hours: Monday-Thursday 7 a.m.-3 p.m., Friday 7 a.m.-2 p.m., Saturday and Sunday closed

Bevo Bucks

Chick-fil-A

Food: chicken

Location: Texas Union

Favorite Dish: chicken nuggets, waffle fries

Hours: Monday-Friday 10:30 a.m.-4 p.m., closed Saturday and Sunday

Bevo Bucks

Commons Coffee Co.

Food: coffee, bagels, muffins

Location: Texas Union

Favorite Dish: bagel and cream cheese, cappuccino

Hours: Monday-Thursday 6 a.m.-6 p.m.,Friday 6 a.m.-5 p.m.

Bevo Bucks

Cypress Bend

Food: convenience store with grill and deli

Location: San Jacinto

Favorite Dish: blackened chicken caesar salad, spicy curly fries

Hours: Monday-Thursday 7 a.m.-8 p.m., Friday 7 a.m.-3 p.m., Saturday and Sunday 12 p.m.-7 p.m.

Dining Dollars and Bevo Bucks

Field of Greens

Food: salads

Location: Texas Union

Favorite Dish: caesar salad

Hours: Monday-Friday 10:30 a.m.-2:30 p.m., closed Saturday and Sunday

Bevo Bucks

Java City

Food: coffee

Location: CBA

Favorite Dish: café mocha

Hours: Monday-Tuesday 7 a.m.-8 p.m., Wednesday-Thursday 7 a.m.-5 p.m., Friday 7 a.m.-3 p.m., closed Saturday and Sunday

Bevo Bucks

Jester City Limits

Food: á la carte cafeteria

Location: Jester

Favorite Dish: Italian classic foccacia sandwich, Krispy Kreme donuts

Hours: Monday-Thursday 7 a.m.-11 p.m., Friday 7 a.m.-9 p.m., Saturday 9 a.m.-8 p.m., Sunday 9 a.m.-11 p.m.

Dining Dollars and Bevo Bucks

Jest'A Pizza

Food: pizza

Location: Jester

Favorite Dish: cheese personal pan pizza

Hours: Monday-Thursday 11 a.m.-12 a.m., Friday 11 a.m.-9 p.m., Saturday 11 a.m.-8 p.m., Sunday 5 p.m.-12 a.m.

Dining Dollars and Bevo Bucks

Jester 2nd Floor Dining Hall

Food: cafeteria-style

Location: Jester

Favorite Dish: ginger orange chicken, french fries, chicken strips

Hours: Monday-Friday Lunch 11:30 a.m.-2 p.m., Dinner 4:30 p.m.-7:30 p.m.

Dining Dollars and Bevo Bucks

Jester Vending Machines

Food: candy, cokes, chips

Location: Jester 1st Floor Concourse

Favorite Dish: Dr. Pepper, Cheetos, Snickers

Hours: 24 Hours

Bevo Bucks

Kins Korner

Food: snacks

Location: Kinsolving

Favorite Dish: Krispy Kreme, slice of pizza, Blue Bell pint

Hours: Monday-Friday 7 a.m.-3 p.m.

Dining Dollars and Bevo Bucks

Kinsolving Dining Hall

Food: cafeteria-style

Location: Kinsolving

Favorite Dish: chicken strips, chicken fried steak

Hours: Monday-Friday Breakfast 7 a.m.-9:30 a.m., Continental Breakfast 9:30 a.m.-10:30 a.m., Lunch 10:30 a.m.-1:30 p.m., Dinner 4:30 p.m.-7:00 p.m., Saturday Brunch 11 a.m.-2 p.m., Dinner 4:30 p.m.-7 p.m., Sunday Lunch 11:00 a.m.-2 p.m.

Dining Dollars and Bevo Bucks

Kinsolving Study Break

Food: grill and snacks

Location: Kinsolving

Favorite Dish: cheeseburger, chicken on a stick

Hours: Monday-Thursday 9 p.m.-12 a.m., Sunday 5 p.m.-12 a.m.

Dining Dollars and Bevo Bucks

Odyssey Café

Food: Greek

Location: Jester

Favorite Dish: Greek Salad

Hours: Monday-Thursday 11 a.m.-8 p.m., Friday 11 a.m.-3 p.m.

Dining Dollars

Taco Bell

Food: Mexican

Location: Texas Union

Favorite Dish: Cheesy Gordita Crunch, soft tacos, 7 Layer Burrito

Hours: Monday-Thursday 10 a.m.-8 p.m., Friday 10 a.m.-7 p.m., Saturday 11 a.m.-5 p.m., Sunday 12 p.m.-5 p.m.

Bevo Bucks

Tortilla Flats

Food: Mexican

Location: Texas Union

Favorite Dish: cheese quesadilla

Hours: Monday-Friday 7:00 a.m.-2:00 p.m., closed Saturday and Sunday

Bevo Bucks

Sports Café

Food: sandwiches, smoothies, drinks

Location: Gregory Gym

Favorite Dish: turkey sandwich, Freshens smoothie

Hours: Monday-Thursday 8 a.m.-5 p.m., Friday 8 a.m.-4 p.m., closed Saturday and Sunday

Bevo Bucks

Sushi Bar

Food: sushi

Location: Texas Union

Favorite Dish: California Roll

Hours: Monday-Friday 10:30 a.m.-2:30 p.m., closed Saturday and Sunday

Bevo Bucks

Sushi Bar

Food: Sushi

Location: Jester

Favorite Dish: California Roll

Hours: Monday-Thursday 10 a.m.-12 a.m., Friday-Saturday 10 a.m.-7 p.m., Sunday 10 a.m.-12 a.m.

Bevo Bucks

Wendy's

Food: burgers

Location: Texas Union

Favorite Dish: bacon cheeseburger, Frosty, fries

Hours: Monday-Friday 7 a.m.- 2 a.m., Saturday 10 a.m.-2 a.m., Sunday 12 p.m.-2 a.m.

Bevo Bucks

Off-Campus Places to Use Your Meal Plan:

Burger King
27th and Guadalupe
(512) 477-5672

Castilian Cordova Café
2323 San Antonio St.
(512) 478-9811

Chipotle
2230 Guadalupe
(512) 320-0238

Dobie Cafeteria
21st and Guadalupe
(512) 505-1000

Domino's Pizza
404 W. 26th St.
(512) 476-7181

Double Dave's
415 W. 24th St.
(512) 472-DAVE

Gumby's
2222 Rio Grande St.
(512) 472-3278

Hoa Hoa Restaurant
Dobie Mall
(512) 505-0155

Jack in the Box
2552 Guadalupe
(512) 474 1708

Jack in the Box
1000 E. 41st St. (Hancock Center)
(512) 458-6252

Jamba Juice
2300 Guadalupe #100
(512) 275-0290

Laundry Mom-Student Laundry Service
(512) 454-9292

Mr. Gatti's
38th and Guadalupe,
503 W. MLK
(512) 459-2222

Niki's Pizza
Dobie Mall
(512) 474-1876

NRG Wireless Solutions
1904 Guadalupe
(512) 473-8702|

Pita Pit
2001 Guadalupe
(512) 480-8600

Pizza Classics
604 W. 29th St.
(512) 320-8080

Pizza Hut
2021B E. Riverside Dr.,
1811 Guadalupe
(512) 444-4444

Pluckers
2222 Rio Grande
(512) 469-WING

Schlotsky's
1915 Guadalupe
(512) 457-1129

Subway
2323 San Antonio
(512) 476-1803

Subway
2900 Guadalupe
(512) 469-2902

Taco Cabana
211 S. Lamar
(512) 472-8098

Taco Cabana
2507 E. Riverside
(512) 462-2236

Taco Cabana
517 W. MLK Blvd
(512) 478-0875

Thai Noodles
Etc., 2602 Guadalupe
(512) 494-1011

Tiff's Treats
(512) 473-2600

Wendy's
413 W. MLK
(512) 482-8456

Wendy's
224 E. Riverside Dr.
(512) 804-1614

Wendy's
3570 Far West Blvd
(512) 795-9598

Wing Zone
907 W. 24th St.
(512) 370-BIRD

Wok This Way
314 W. 17th St.
(512) 473-2WOK

24-Hour Dining:
No

Student Favorites:
Wendy's, Chick-fil-A

Did You Know?

The Castilian (a private dorm one block off campus) rated Cordova Café the 3rd best cafeteria in Austin behind Luby's and Furr's a few years ago. Residents and non-residents with Bevo Bucks, who buy a meal plan, or who pay the per-meal rate, can enjoy the **all-you-can-eat breakfast, lunch and dinner buffet** 7 days a week.

You can **use your Bevo Bucks at non-food places** on campus, such as the UT Duplicating Service and the UT Learning Center.

Other Options

There are egg roll stands on Guadalupe in front of the Co-op and Barnes and Noble, and on 21st Street in front of Littlefield Fountain with lots of cheap food options. Double Dave's has a catering truck in front of the PCL where you can grab a slice of pizza between classes.

Other stands include Groundhog Coffee Carts (21st & Speedway, Law School), Pato's Tacos (East & West of RLM on 26th), Arturo's II (Doty Fine Arts Center), Speedway Coffee Company (24th & Speedway, RLM), University Coffee Company (University and W. Dean Keeton, 23rd and San Jacinto, and Communications Plaza), and O's to Go (24th and Speedway). In addition to these, there is Subway in the Law School, O's Restaurant at 24th and Speedway, as well as the Dobie Food Court, which has many different options.

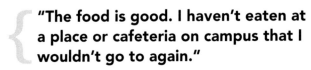

Students Speak Out On...
Campus Dining

> "The food is good. I haven't eaten at a place or cafeteria on campus that I wouldn't go to again."

Q "I have heard the **Kinsolving dining hall is the best for on-campus dining**. I have no idea. The Union has the traditional: Wendy's and Chick-fil-A. Never buy food from a food cart on campus! That is sick and wrong."

Q "Kinsolving is the best, **the Union is solid, but costs more than dining halls** (Bevo Bucks rule!). Philly cheese or chicken strips are where it's at in Jester."

Q "The Union is definitely the way to go. There are many different options. **Tortilla Flats, and Chick-fil-A are favorites**. I have tried Bene Pizza, and while it looks like it is really good, I didn't particularly like it. Texadelphia in the Union Underground or just on the Drag is also always a great choice—you can't really go wrong there. There is a Wendy's in the Union and Burger King in the business school. However, a lot of them are only open a few hours every day, so if you like to eat at odd hours, watch out. That applies to dining halls, too: be sure to watch their hours of operation if you don't want to go hungry or have to go out to eat. The good thing about Dining Dollars and Bevo Bucks is that if your dining hall is closed, you can use your money somewhere else without actually having to use cash."

Q "Campus food is still 'campus food.' It is edible, but other locations and restaurants serve better quality food. My **two favorite restaurants in Austin are Chuy's and Magnolia Café**."

Q "There is a variety of foods available in the Union. **Jester has a major cafeteria, but Kinsolving usually provides better food**, or at least cheap food. Unbeknownst to most people is the Burger King in the business school atrium."

Q "I believe the food on campus is normal **relative to most dorm cafeterias**. Thank God I did not live in an on-campus dorm and never had to experience that nastiness. The Castilian, one of the private dorms off-campus, is known for its great food."

Q "Who knows how the food is on campus? **Yay for private dorms**!"

Q "The food is excellent. **Texadelphia in the Union Underground on Saturdays is the best**!"

Q "**I eat at Taco Bell because they serve cheap food**. When the other places on campus agree that cheap food is good, I will include them in my list of good spots."

Q "My personal favorite is O's Café because it is not expensive, and it is fairly good. Jester dorm food has mixed reviews, and **if you are into salad bars, I don't recommend going there**."

Q "The food on campus is great and usually cheap. Good spots are Taco Bell and the eggroll cart on 21st Street by the South Mall. **It's heaven in styrofoam**!"

Q "The Union has great fast food restaurants and delis. Just remember that Chick-fil-A is always closed on Sundays—it will save you some disappointment in the future if you go there just to ease your craving for chicken. Castilian dorm has great food and daily grill specials. **They have birthday dinners every month and you get steak on your birthday month**."

Q "**Food on campus is okay**. All I eat on campus is fast food from the Union and Dobie Mall (right across the street from campus). I don't ever eat at the dining halls, so I don't know much about them."

The College Prowler Take On...
Campus Dining

Overall, not many people love dorm food, especially on-campus dorm food. Some of the private dorms, such as SRD and Castilian, have pretty good food, but for the most part, Bevo Bucks are the best way to go because they can be used at so many places. The Union is a good bet with many different choices, and Wendy's is open late, so you can "Eat Great, Even Late." Jest'A Pizza is a good option. Even though dining hall food may not be your favorite, there is always something to eat because there are so many choices. Even as a vegetarian, there are always plenty of options—though you'll never be on the Atkins diet because the vegetarian options are mostly carbs.

Students seem to agree that Kinsolving may have the best dining hall on campus. San Jacinto is the newest dorm and has a fairly good reputation for dorm food. Jester's dining hall gets mixed reviews. A great way to make your on-campus dining experience the best that it can be is with Bevo Bucks. With your on-campus housing contract you are given $300 of Bevo Bucks; however, It's recommended that you purchase more because Bevo Bucks can be used at so many different restaurants on and around campus. Then, when you get sick of dorm food, you have many other options.

B

The College Prowler® Grade on
Campus Dining: B

Our grade on Campus Dining addresses the quality of both school-owned dining halls and independent on-campus restaurants as well as the price, availability, and variety of food.

Off-Campus Dining

The Lowdown On...
Off-Campus Dining

Restaurant Prowler:
Popular Places to Eat!

El Arroyo

Food: Mexican

Address: 1024 W. 5th St.

(512) 474-1222

Cool Features: Pat Green sings about it

Price: $15 and under per person

Hours: Sunday-Thursday 11 a.m.-10 p.m., Friday-Saturday 11 a.m.-12 a.m.

The Cheesecake Factory

Food: American

Address: 10000 Research Blvd.

(512) 241-0777

Cool Features: List of 36 different cheesecakes from which to choose

Price: $25 and under per person

Hours: Monday-Thursday 11 a.m.-11 p.m., Friday-Saturday 11 a.m.-12:30 a.m., Sunday 10 a.m.-11 p.m.

Try: orange chicken, pad Thai noodles, the club, chinese chicken salad

Chuy's

Food: Mexican

Address: 1728 Barton Springs

(512) 474-4452

Cool Features: The decorations are very original with lots of Elvis. Your silverware comes wrapped in plastic with a dot sticker, so you can write your name or a message on the sticker and stick it on the ceiling. Best salsa in town!!!

Price: $15 and under per person

Hours: Sunday-Thursday 11 a.m.-10:30 p.m., Friday-Saturday 11 a.m.-11 p.m.

Try: banditos, enchiladas with deluxe sauce, great salsa!

Dirty Martin's

Food: burgers

Address: 2808 Guadalupe

(512) 477-3173

Cool Features: an Austin landmark since 1926

Price: $10 and under per person

Hours: Monday-Sunday 11 a.m.-11 p.m.

Try: Sissy Burger, onion rings, and a chocolate shake

EZ's

Food: American

Address: 3918 N. Lamar Blvd.

(512) 302-1800

Cool Features: Discount with your student ID

(EZ's, continued)

Price: $15 and under per person

Hours: Sunday-Saturday 11 a.m.-11 p.m.

Try: margherita pizza, chocolate shake

Freebird's Burrito

Food: Burritos/quesadillas

Address: 41st and Red River, Hancock Shopping Center

(512) 451-5514

Price: $10 and under per person

Hours: Sunday-Thursday 11 a.m.-10:30 p.m., Friday-Saturday 11 a.m.-11 p.m.

Try: quesadilla with guacamole—it comes on the inside, rather than on top, yummy!

Hula Hut

Food: Mexican/Polynesian

Address: 3825 Lake Austin Blvd.

(512) 476-4852

Cool Features: On the shore of Lake Austin, nice views, excellent salsa—same as Chuys!

Price: $20 and under per person

Hours: Sunday-Thursday 11 a.m.-10 p.m., Friday-Saturday 11 a.m.-11 p.m.

Try: the Hulala—a drink in a fishbowl, Shiner Bock fajitas, coconut shrimp

Katz's Deli and Bar

Food: deli, sandwiches, American, breakfast

Address: 618 W. 6th St.

(512) 472-2037

Cool Features: pick-up service, happy hour in the morning from 7-11, and again from 4-7 p.m.

Price: $15-20 and under per person

Hours: 24 hours a day

Try: reuben, matzo ball soup, bagel with lox, fried pickles, cheesecake shake

Kerbey Lane Café

Food: American, breakfast, Mexican

Address: 2606 Guadalupe

(512) 477-5717

Price: $15 and under per person

Hours: 24 hours a day

Try: Kerbey Queso, pancake of the day, baked potato omelet

Magnolia Café

Food: American/Mexican/Breakfast

Address: 2304 Lake Austin Blvd.

(512) 478-8645

Cool Features: very cheap

Price: $10 and under per person

Hours: 24 hours a day

Try: Mag Mud queso, flamingo sandwich, potato landscape, omelets

Mustache Pete's

Food: pizza

Address: 415 W. 24th St.

(412) 447-7383

Cool Features: all-you-can-eat buffet every day for $5.99, happy hour 4-7 p.m. daily with $1.00 selected drafts

Price: $10 and under per person

Hours: Sunday-Thursday 11 a.m.-10 p.m., Friday-Saturday 11 a.m.-10 p.m.

Try: pepperoni rolls, dessert pizza

The Oasis

Food: American/Mexican

Address: 6550 Comanche Trail

(512) 266-2441

Cool Features: high above Lake Travis. beautiful views of the sunset, outdoor patio seating

Price: $20 and under per person

Hours: Monday-Saturday 11:30 a.m.-10 p.m., Sunday 10:30 a.m.-10 p.m.

Try: fajitas, cheeseburger

The Omelettry

Food: American/breakfast

Address: 4811 Burnet Rd.

(512) 453-5062

Cool Features: small and funky, cash only

Price: $10 and under per person

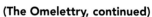

(The Omelettry, continued)
Hours: Sunday-Monday
7 a.m.-5 p.m.

Try: chocolate chip pancakes, guacamole omelet; Nestle Quik chocolate milk is also available.

Player's
Food: burgers
Address: 300 W. MLK Blvd
(512) 478-9299
Cool Features: open late, sports bar
Price: $10 and under per person
Hours: Sunday-Thursday 10:45 a.m.-3 a.m., Friday-Saturday 10:45 a.m.-3:30 a.m.
Try: veggie burger, fried mushrooms

Romano's Macaroni Grill
Food: Italian
Address: 701 Capital of Texas Hwy. Building K
(512) 329-0000
Cool Features: Large wine list
Price: $20 and under per person
Hours: Daily Lunch 11 a.m.-4p.m., Dinner Monday-Thursday4 p.m.-10 p.m., Friday-Saturday 4 p.m.-11 p.m.

Salt Lick BBQ
Food: BBQ
Address: 18001 FM 1826 Driftwood, Texas
(512) 894-3117
Cool Features: BYOB, all-you-can-eat family-style dining available
Price: $20 and under per person
Hours: Sunday-Saturday 11 a.m.-10 p.m.
Try: Brisket, Ribs

Suzi's China Grill
Food: Chinese and sushi
Address: 7858 Shoal Creek Blvd.
(512) 302-4600
Price: $20 and under per person
Hours: Monday-Thursday 11 a.m.-10 p.m., Friday-Saturday 11 a.m.-11 p.m.
Try: shrimp lo mein, Alaska roll, Philly roll

Scholz Bier Garten
(pronounced Schultz's)
Food: American
Address: 1607 San Jacinto Blvd.
(512) 474-1958
Cool Features: oldest restaurant and bier garten in Texas—1866, 30 draft beer taps, outside patio, very popular on game days

(Scholz Bier Garten, continued)

Price: $15 and under
per person

Hours: Sunday-Saturday
11 a.m.-10 p.m.,

Try: chicken fried steak, BBQ
brisket, bratwurst

Texadelphia

Food: cheesesteak
sandwiches, queso

Address: 2422 Guadalupe St.

(512) 480-0107

Cool Features: cheap beers,
on the drag

Price: $10 and under
per person

Hours: Sunday-Saturday
11 a.m.-9 p.m.

Try: cheesesteak sandwich with
mustard, veggie sandwich,
queso with guacamole added

Texas French Bread

Food: Sandwiches, Bakery

Address: 2900 Rio Grande

(512) 499-0544

Cool Features: loaves of bread
and cakes to go

Price: $10 and under
per person

Hours: Monday-Friday
6:30 a.m.-6:30 p.m., Saturday-
Sunday 7 a.m.-5 p.m.

Try: Vegetarian Sandwich,
La Nicoise Sandwich, Turkey
Sandwich, Pasta Salad

(Texas French Bread, continued)

The Lunch Special: half a
sandwich, soup of the day or
salad (green, fruit, or pasta),
drink and a cookie

Trudy's Texas Star

Food: Mexican

Address: 409 West 30th

(512) 477-2935

www.trudys.com

Cool Features: upstairs
restaurant with bar, downstairs
bar with appetizers. Also
serves breakfast. Get the
Mexican martini—these are the
most famous in town, and they
have a limit of two.

Price: $15 and under
per person

Hours: Monday-Thursday
11 a.m.-12 a.m., bar open until
2 a.m., Friday 11 a.m.-2 a.m.
Saturday-Sunday 9 a.m.-2 a.m.

Try: Mexican martini, Texas star
nachos, flaquities

West Lynn Café

Food: Vegetarian

Address: 1110 W Lynn St.

(512) 482-0950

Cool Features: great wine list

Price: $12 - $15 per person

Hours: Tuesday-Thursday
11:30 a.m.-10 p.m., Friday
11:30 a.m. -10:30 p.m.,
Saturday 11 a.m.-10:30 p.m.,
Sunday 11 a.m.-9:30 p.m.

Try: mushroom walnut crepes

Student Favorites:

Chuy's

Hula Hut

Trudy's

Magnolia Café

Texadelphia

Late-Night Dining:

Amy's Ice Cream

Cain and Abel's (see Nightlife section)

Jack in the Box

Jimmy John's

Player's

Plucker's

Taco Bell

24-Hour Eating:

Burger King drive-thru

Katz's Deli

Ken's Donuts

Kerbey Lane Café

IHOP

Magnolia Café

Star Seeds

Taco Cabana

Whataburger

Other Places to Check Out:

Hudson's on the Bend

Texas Land & Game Cattle Co.

Rosie's Taqueria

Closest Grocery Stores:

Randall's - between 34th and 38th just west of Lamar

HEB - 41st and Red River-Hancock Shopping Center

Central Market - 38th and Lamar

Best Pizza:

Gumby's

Pizza Hut

Best Chinese:

Suzi's China Grill

Best Breakfast:

The Omelettry

Magnolia Café

Best Wings:

Plucker's

Wing Zone

Best Healthy:

West Lynn Café

Central Market

Zen Japanese

Best Place to Take Your Parents:

The Oasis

Best Burger:
Dirty Martin's
Hula Hut
Player's

Best Mexican:
Chuy's
Trudy's Texas Star

Best Fast Food:
Taco Bell

Best Ice Cream:
Amy's Ice Cream

Best Place to Cure a Hangover:
Texadelphia

Best BBQ:
Salt Lick BBQ

Best Cheap Food:
Magnolia Café

Best Italian:
Romano's Macaroni Grill

Best Buffet:
Mustache Pete's

Students Speak Out On...
Off-Campus Dining

> "Lots of food is available off campus. Magnolia Café is a cheap favorite. Other notables include Texadelphia, and the Omelettry for breakfast. Jamba Juice is a great way to enjoy a sunny afternoon."

Q "There are so many places to choose from! At least once a year, you must **pack up your friends and a cooler of beer to go to the Salt Lick, southwest of Austin**. They have the best BBQ and sides for $15 all-you-can-eat. It's BYOB, and there's usually live music."

Q "Restaurants off-campus are amazing. **Tex-mex is very popular**—Chuy's, Trudy's, Hula Hut. Other great places to eat include Magnolia, and Freebirds."

Q "There are tons of fun places off campus; Chuy's, Macaroni Grill, Hula Hut, and Trudy's are just a few great places that I like (some chains, some not). **They all vary in genre, atmosphere, and price**."

Q "**Dirty Martin's has the best milkshakes ever**! Kerbey Lane Café is good 24 hours a day—never forget that. When your parents are in town, the Oasis and the Cheesecake Factory are good places for them to pay for. Buffalo wings are their own food group: there is a wing shop on nearly every corner in West Campus."

Q "The restaurants off campus are good. **I've heard Austin has the most restaurants per capita in the U.S.**, so there's always a good choice. Some of my favorites are Chuy's and Hula Hut."

Q "There are so many great places to eat in Austin. **Trudy's is by far my favorite**—great food, atmosphere, and strong drinks (Mexican Martini). Texadelphia is always a favorite."

Q "**Austin is full of restaurants**. If you ask 25 people for their favorite spot, you will probably get close to 20 different answers."

Q "Chuy's, Hula Hut, plus the late night Taco C, Jimmy John's, Plucker's, and Gumby's are **all worth checking out**. There are a bunch of great restaurants here."

Q "**It's hit or miss with Chinese food along the Drag**. Don't forget that usually you get what you pay for with Mexican food. Tiff's Treats are the reason for the Freshman 15: the most amazing cookies ever, and the delivery guys are all cute. They're great for last-minute birthday gifts or study break. Plus, they can be sent anonymously!"

Q "Austin restaurants have the best Tex-Mex food around—great food and great atmospheres! **Don't forget to share a Hulala at Hula Hut, or get a Mag Mud at Magnolia Café**."

Q "The restaurants off-campus are wonderful. My all-time favorite is the Oasis on the East shore of Lake Travis (by 2222 and 620). The food is good and the atmosphere is worth the sometimes-pricey menu. **Freebirds off Red River serves cheap, great burritos**."

Q "Tons of places in Austin are good. I like **Dirty's, EZ's, Rudy's, the Salt Lick** . . . the list goes on."

Q "Magnolia Café is my favorite. It's 24/7, and the first time I went there was at 2 a.m. **They were rockin' out to the Fugees and Tupac**. If your waiter or cook does not have tattoos or colored hair, something is wrong—but don't be afraid, they're all great! If you like exotic meats, or just plain good food, sucker your parents into taking you to Hudson's on the Bend off 620 in the hills. They serve things like Rattlesnake Cakes, Ostrich, Lobster-stuffed Venison, and much more wild game. Texas Land & Cattle Co. has great steak for a more moderate budget. For Willie Nelson's favorite Tex-Mex, head out to Rosie's Taqueria on 71, just past 620."

The College Prowler Take On...
Off-Campus Dining

Food in Austin is awesome! One of the best things about this town is the sheer number of restaurants, not to mention the quality of our restaurants. Austin is home to tons of great Mexican restaurants, and those are definitely student favorites. A favorite Austin pastime is Mexican food and a nice cold margarita . . . or just the margarita. Some of the best in town are found at Iron Cactus, Trudy's, Nuevo Leon, El Arroyo and Baby Acapulco (Baby A's). If you want to get really drunk, try the Purple at Baby A's or the Cactus Juice at Iron Cactus (it is made with everclear), or the Mexican martinis at Trudys (there is a limit of two).

Austin has every other type of food you can imagine from BBQ to Thai, Chinese to tapas, delis to vegetarian-only. There are so many places to try, and the students recommend Magnolia Café, Dirty's, Texadelphia, Hula Hut and Freebird's. The most popular things to do in Austin besides go to 6th Street, frat parties, or protest, is to go out to eat. So, get ready to gain your Freshman 15 here in Austin and find your new favorite restaurants.

The College Prowler® Grade on

Off-Campus
Dining: A

A high off-campus dining grade implies that off-campus restaurants are affordable, accessible, and worth visiting. Other factors include the variety of cuisine and the availability of alternative options (vegetarian, vegan, Kosher, etc.).

Campus Housing

The Lowdown On...
Campus Housing

Room Types:
Single, Double, Triple

Best Dorms:
On Campus:
San Jacinto

Private Dorms:
Coed - Castilian, Towers,
Girls Only - Hardin House, SRD

Worst Dorms:
Jester (Though some would
argue that this is the best dorm
because of the number of
people and the location.)

Dobie is nice, but antisocial.

Dormitories:
11 on campus, 7 private

Undergrads on Campus:
Freshman 70%
Others 18%

→

Dormitories:

Brackenridge

Floors: 4

Total Occupancy: 122

Bathrooms: Community

Coed: Yes

Room Types: Double, single, one triple

Special Features: Brackenridge was built in 1933 and is actually the second Brackenridge. The first was built in 1890 in the spot where Welch Hall now stands. It burned down in 1952. Brackenridge offers moveable, bunkable beds in the rooms, as well as study areas, a TV room, pool table, foosball and ping-pong table for the residents.

Honors Residence

Andrews/Blanton/Carothers

Floors: 4/5/4

Total Occupancy: 492

Bathrooms: Community

Coed: Yes

Room Types: Double

Special Features: Some rooms have built-in furniture, some have movable furniture, wood floors, and most have a vanity area with sink. The dorms also have amenities such as an elevator, computer lab, piano, washer, dryer and ironing board on every floor, study rooms, multi purpose rooms, three sundecks, and TV lounges.

(Honors Residence, continued)

The Honors Residence provides extra-curricular programming for its residents, and there is a shared courtyard for cookouts, games and relaxation. You must be invited to live there by the University as it is for Honors Students. Those who live there call it the Quad.

Jester Center

Floors: 14

Total Occupancy: 2,912

Bathrooms: Some community, some connecting, both types of bathrooms in both towers of Jester

Coed: Yes

Room Types: Double rooms, some triples

Special Features: Jester was built in 1969, is by far the largest dorm on campus and consists of two towers, Jester East and Jester West. The dorm rooms contain built-in furniture and a vanity area with sink. Some of the amenities of Jester include an elevator, study rooms, a piano room, big screen TV room, game room, many dining options, lounge areas, activity room, weight room, lawn area, computer labs, and a convenience store on site.

Kinsolving

Floors: 3

Total Occupancy: 761

Bathrooms: Some connecting baths, some community baths

Coed: No

Percentage of Men/Women*: 0%/100%
*During the summer, provisional students live in Kinsolving, and it operates as a coed dorm.

Room Types: Double

Special Features: Kinsolving was built in 1958, and it's the larger of the two all-girl dorms on campus. Each room has built-in furniture and its own vanity area with sink. Kinsolving features sitting and study areas on every floor, as well as laundry facilities on every floor. Residents can enjoy a recreation room, weight room, two large lounges for watching TV, dining facilities, elevator, piano, computer lab and a sundeck.

Littlefield

Floors: 3

Total Occupancy: 157

Bathrooms: Community

Coed: No

Percentage of Men/Women: 0%/100%

Room Types: Double, one single

(Littlefield, continued)

Special Features: Littlefield is UT's oldest dorm, built in 1926. Littlefield has back verandas for relaxing, studying and visiting with friends, a living room with a baby grand piano, an elevator, a TV room, and every floor has a washer, dryer, and ironing board. The rooms have movable furniture, a vanity area with sink, bunkable beds, and a built-in dresser.

Moore-Hill

Floors: 5

Total Occupancy: 390

Bathrooms: Community

Coed: No

Percentage of Men/Women: 100%/0%

Room Types: Double, 2 single rooms

Special Features: Moore-Hill Hall is actually two residence Halls attached to each other (Moore Hall and Hill Hall). There are some rooms with moveable furniture and bunkable beds and other rooms have built-in furniture. Residents can play ping-pong, and foosball, throw darts, use vending machines, study rooms, or watch TV in the TV lounge.

Prather

Floors: 5

Total Occupancy: 156

Bathrooms: Community

Coed: No

Percentage of Men/Women: 100%/0%

Room Types: Double

Special Features: The rooms at Prather offer moveable furniture. Residents can spend time in the TV lounge, study areas, and computer lab and laundry facilities are also available.

Roberts

Floors: 4

Total Occupancy: 32 at most

Bathrooms: Community

Coed: Yes

Room Types: Double and single

Special Features: If you want a very small dorm community experience, Roberts is the dorm for you. Roberts separates men and women into clusters of eight rooms each. The very small number of residents makes for a very bonded group of residents. The rooms have moveable furniture, and the dorm has a living room, laundry facilities, study lounges and a TV room.

San Jacinto

Floors: 5

Total Occupancy: 866

Bathrooms: All rooms have a private bath

Coed: Yes

Room Types: Double

Special Features: San Jacinto was built in 2000, and it's the newest dorm on the UT campus. The rooms have moveable furniture with loftable/bunkable beds, and each room contains a vanity area with a sink. San Jacinto has many amenities that other dorms do not, such as an outdoor amphitheater, game room, the Leather Lounge, laundry facilities, vending areas, computer lab, study lounges, and a convenience store with a grill and deli.

Simkins

Floors: 3

Total Occupancy: 197

Bathrooms: Community

Coed: No

Percentage of Men/Women: 100%/0%

Room Types: Double

Special Features: Simkins is located away from most of the other dorms and is near the engineering school, law school and fine arts building. Rooms have moveable/bunkable beds, some have partially built-in furniture and/or a vanity area with sink. Some cool amenities are a kitchenette, an outdoor sand volleyball court and a 24-hour study room, as well as the standard computer lab, laundry facilities, and a recreation area.

→

Whitis Court

Floors: 2

Total Occupancy: 100

Bathrooms: Community

Coed: Yes

Special Features: The Whitis Court dorms are a special place for the Residential FIGS program-students to live and interact with other first-year students who take the same classes that they do. Within Whitis Court there are classroom and conference room facilities for academic purposes, spacious living, study and social areas within each building, laundry facilities, and kitchenettes. There are single sex and coed areas of the dorm, and the rooms come with desks, dressers, closets and bunkable and loftable beds.

Other University Owned Housing:

University Apartments for student families (about six miles from campus), the Brackenridge Apartments, Colorado Apartments, and Gateway Apartments where there are one-, two-, and three-bedroom aparments available.

Amenities: playgrounds, laundry facilities, cable TV hookups, on bus routes, 24-hour University police patrol, parking

Private Dorms:

Castilian

Floors: 22, 11 floors of residence, 9 floors of parking

Total Occupancy: 704

Bathrooms: Private, suites share bath

Coed: Yes

Room Types: 4 person suites

Special Features: Castilian was built in the 1960s, and was completely refurbished in the summer of 2003. Amenities include an indoor swimming pool, 24-hour service desk, quiet study lounge, unlimited dining, resident activities, tanning bed, rooftop sun deck, TV rooms on every floor, a large TV lounge on the main floor, workout room, game room with pool tables, computer lab, covered parking, and on-site laundry. The rooms come with moveable furniture, desks, dressers, closets, high-speed Internet access, cable, microwave, mini fridge and housekeeping. Castilian also provides roommate-matching service. Castilian is located one block off campus, and is by far the most social dorm—you'll meet a ton of people.

→

Contessa

Floors: 4

Total Occupancy:

Bathrooms: Private

Coed: Yes

Room Types: Single, double

Special Features: Contessa has three different buildings with different floorplans: Contessa West, Contessa East and Barrone. The rooms are large and some have a living area, breakfast area, and kitchenette, while others are simply a bedroom and bathroom. Contessa has two pools, TV lounge, study rooms, lounges, computer rooms, laundry room, exercise room, and recreation area.

Dobie

Floors: 27

Total Occupancy: 940

Bathrooms: Private

Coed: Yes

Room Types: Efficiency, studio, studio plus, side suite, corner suite, corner suite plus, private studio

Special Features: Dobie was built in 1971 and offers a multimedia computer center, study rooms on floors three through 13, free printing in the computer lab, 24-hour quiet floors, on-site maintenance and housekeeping staffs, and numerous social programs for its residents. Dobie also provides educational programs for its residents, has facilities open 24 hours a day such as a fitness center, game room, mini theater TV room, pool and spa, and basketball and volleyball courts. In addition, Dobie sits on top of Dobie Mall which includes the Dobie Movie Theatre, Powerplay Arcade, Ticket City, and several stores such as Gumballs Candy Store and Jewel Cove, as well as a food court.

→

Hardin House

Floors: 2

Total Occupancy: 223

Bathrooms: Private, connecting

Coed: No

Percentage of Men/Women: 0%/100%

Room Types: Mostly double, some single and triple

Special Features: Hardin House opened in 1937 and has been THE address for girls to live since then. Hardin House has five different buildings: Main, Red and Red Annex, Green, Grant and the Apartments, and each have varying floor plans. Hardin House offers great meals, 24-hour manned front desk, housekeeping, all bills paid (except phone and Internet), two pools, garden and patio areas, on-site parking, TV lounges, exercise rooms, computer and study rooms, high-speed Internet access and cable TV.

Madison House

Floors: 3

Total Occupancy: more than 215

Bathrooms: Private, connecting

Coed: Yes

Room Types: two- and three-bedroom suites, one- and two-bedroom apartments

Special Features: Madison House, Madison Three and the Bellaire Apartments have a pool, game room, fitness room, and optional meal plans.

Scottish Rite Dormitory

Floors: 3

Total Occupancy:

Bathrooms: Community, connecting

Coed: No

Percentage of Men/Women: 0%/100%

Room Types: Double and single

Special Features: SRD was built in 1922 on 7 acres of land on the North side of campus and is the other all-girls private dorm. Amenities offered by SRD are a fitness center with group classes (such as Pilates, kickboxing), Internet connections and computer lab, swimming pool and resident activities. SRD is also known for its great food and is the only residence hall on campus that maintains a library for the use of its residents.

→

University Towers

Floors: 10

Total Occupancy: 600

Bathrooms: Private, Connecting

Coed: Yes

Room Types: Apartment style—two bedroom, living room, kitchen

Special Features: Towers offers apartment-style living, with large living areas, large bedrooms, private bathrooms with oversized vanities, walk-in closets, private balconies, kitchens with full-size refrigerators and microwaves, range tops and garbage disposals, air conditioning, heating and hot water controls in every suite, two phone and Ethernet hookups in each bedroom, and cable. There are laundry facilities on every floor, housekeeping service, TV lounges on every floor, 24-hour computer lab, intercom admittance and courtesy patrol, game room and workout room, as well as social events for the residents.

Housing Types Offered:

Singles: 3%
Doubles: 87%
Apartments: 10%

Available for Rent

Nothing, but you are provided with a microwave and fridge.

Bed Type

Extra-long twin, except Littlefield and Kinsolving-Twin

Note: An idea many students come up with is to buy a full/queen blanket for their twin beds. The blanket covers any mess stored underneath the bed and saves the students from buying another blanket when they move off campus into an apartment with a full/queen bed.

Cleaning Service?

No, not in on campus dorms. Though community bathrooms are cleaned, private rooms are not. Community areas of on-campus dorms are cleaned. Private dorms have maids who come in about once a week and empty your trash cans and vacuum if they can get to your floor.

What You Get

It depends on dorm, see each individual dorm. All halls have study rooms, TV rooms, cable TV and Internet access (ResNet), mircofridge, and laundry rooms.

Also Available

Wellness/Substance-free floor, Residential FIGs (Freshman Interest Groups), College of Engineering Peer Mentor Program

Coed Living

There are both single sex and coed dorms on campus. The coed dorms may be coed by floor, by section of the floor, or by room. The off-campus dorms are either coed or single sex female dorms. There are no private all male dorms. The off-campus dorms are coed by suite or room. Guys and girls will not share a connecting bathroom, but will be across the hall from each other.

Food to Have in Your Dorm (Apartment):

- Easy Mac

- Ramen

- Bottled water or a Brita filtered water pitcher

- Fruit snacks

- Non-perishable items

- Granola bars

- Beef jerky

- Peanut butter

- Saltines and/or bread (for after drinking and/or for stomachaches)

- Powdered drink mix (Gatorade, lemonade)

- Popcorn

- Trail mix

- Hot Pockets

- Jolly Ranchers

Did You Know?

Jester Dorm has its own zip code and is the largest dorm in the nation.

San Jacinto is the newest dorm on campus and was built in 2000.

Littlefield is the oldest dorm on campus and was built in 1926.

The original Brackenridge dorm was built in 1890 and **burned down in 1952** and stood where Welch is today. The second and current Brackenridge was built in 1933.

Students Speak Out On...
Campus Housing

> **"San Jacinto is considered by most to be the best on-campus place to live. It has a great location and big, clean rooms. It's a little like a hospital with the set-up, but it's probably the best on-campus spot."**

Q "I didn't live in an on-campus dorm, but I've heard that Jester is bad, and San Jacinto is good. I lived in University Towers off campus on 24th Street, and it looks and **feels like a gigantic prison**. It's apartment-style, but it's a dorm. All the staff there, except for the RAs are a$$holes, which is probably why nobody lives there anymore."

Q **"Live at Castilian, and don't even bother looking anywhere else**. Everyone I know have always had positive living experiences there."

Q **"If you have a crazy roommate, don't be afraid to ask your RA for a transfer**. If it is going to make you miserable for the rest of the year, you should do something about it. It's not worth ruining your entire freshman year over."

Q **"Always leave your door open at the beginning of freshman year** so that you can meet everyone on your floor. Believe me, people will come in if your door is open. Talk to everyone you can, and don't just wait for people to talk to you. Freshman year is the time to meet people and the dorm is the optimal place to do that, so meet everyone that you can. Try to be friends with lots of people, on your floor and have big floor parties because those are always fun. We would always take over the TV room on our floor and play drinking games together, and it was great. There was also Dance Party 1726."

Q "Everyone should live at Castilian. There is no way I would have lived anywhere else. It is the most fun dorm, it is very convenient to campus, and there is no worrying about community bathrooms. **You can purchase a parking permit and have covered parking all year round**. The food is good in the Cordova Café; they have a big salad bar, a grill where you can get burgers, grilled chicken, veggie burgers, and grilled cheese. One day is stir-fry day, another is quesadilla day, and they have deli meats and cheeses to make sandwiches, various hot foods like french fries, chicken dishes, meat loaf, vegetables, shrimp, and pretty much anything you can think of. If there is anything else you want, you can request it, and they will probably make it. They also usually have things like cottage cheese and frozen yogurt. They always have cold cereal and oatmeal, hot chocolate, Cokes, juices, coffee, and teas. Castilian also has fun events for their residents like 'Casino Night' and 'Friends in Low Places.' You are sure to meet tons of fun people at Castilian. I know I did, and you will have the time of your life. Everyone leaves his or her door open, so it is a very social environment. And very often, your floor and other floors will party together in your TV room, which is in the middle of each floor and has a TV and couches."

Q "Never stayed at any on-campus dorm. From what I hear, **I missed out** because of it!"

Q "Jester sucks. **Prather is quiet as hell, but you can get away with anything there**. Moore-Hill is similar. Live in either Towers or Castilian because you'll have the most fun and you will meet more people there. Get an apartment on West campus after freshman year."

Q "Jester Center has a funky smell to it, but you get used to after a while. **San Jacinto is the lap of luxury, but it's more isolated**."

Q "Basically you want to live in an off-campus dorm. They are literally across the street from campus, so **it's like living on campus, but in a much, much nicer place**. Try the Castilian, Dobie, or Towers. They actually don't cost that much more than living on campus."

Q "Jester is the 'scary dorm,' but it's not that bad (if you don't have a community bath). San Jacinto is really quiet. For private dorms, the Castilian rocks. Towers is cool, but definitely a party spot. Then you have some **good all-girls dorms; SRD, and Hardin House—a.k.a. sorority central**."

Q "For girls, **if you live in a coed setting, it is much easier to make guy friends**. If you are living in an all-girls dorm, your main option for meeting guys is in a party atmosphere. That lends itself more to a dating or hooking up scenario rather than to a friend situation. It is harder to get to know guys on a friend level at parties. However, when you live with them in your dorm, you can make some great guy friends. This should actually work for guys making girl friends, as well."

Q "Each dorm, and each year, has its **own personality**."

Q "I have heard that Jester is actually not that bad considering the size. In fact, **one can make many friends there**."

Q "Castilian has dorm competitions where each floor compete against each other to win a trip to the Salt Lick. They also have parties like **Casino Night and a bonfire party at a ranch**. Most of the RAs are really great. Our RA played April Fool's tricks on almost everyone on the hall. It was hysterical. Sometimes I think maybe I should have lived on campus to be more involved with the University . . . but then I remember I only had to share a bathroom with three other girls."

The College Prowler Take On...
Campus Housing

San Jacinto is the clear favorite of the on-campus dorms, and because it's the newest, it is obvious why. However, almost everyone who applies for on-campus housing is going to put San Jacinto as his/her first choice. Obviously everyone can't live there, so you will have to consider a few back-up choices. Jester is where a majority of people live, and most say it's really not as bad as it seems. But if you do live in Jester, ask for the connecting bathrooms rather than the community bathrooms. Kinsolving and Littlefield are really not bad choices either for girls who do not want to go coed. There are several male single sex dorms as well, Moore-Hill probably being the most well known. However, coed dorms are a lot of fun and teach you a lot about the opposite sex. Some of my best friends are guys because of living in a coed dorm.

If you can afford to live in a private dorm, I highly recommend it, as do many other students. Castilian is a very popular choice. It is coed, a place where you will meet tons of people and have the time of your life—a freshman year that everyone wishes to have. Some dorms have lame RAs who are more strict than others. Well, let me tell you that I knew all of the RAs at Castilian quite well, and they were all very, very cool. Having a good RA is one thing that can completely enhance your freshman year dorm experience. Many girls choose to live in Hardin House or SRD (you must know a Mason to get into SRD). The only downside to those two dorms is that they can be a little bit stuck up. However, if you are cool with that, or want to be around your sorority sisters, those are the places to be.

Towers is more like apartment-style living, since you have a living room and small kitchen. But since you have so much room in your dorm room, you are not forced to go outside of it like you are in Castilian, so you do not meet as many people. There is generally a large Jewish population at Towers, but it attracts all kinds—Greeks and Non-Greeks, the studious to the stoners. Dobie is an off-campus dorm that is very popular with minorities and International students. It does not have a social dorm atmosphere. However, Dobie offers many different types of floor plans, so if you like to have a lot of choices, you might look into living there. Madison and Contessa are not as popular but are other options to check out.

B-

The College Prowler® Grade on

Campus Housing: B-

A high Campus Housing grade indicates that dorms are clean, well-maintained, and spacious. Other determining factors include variety of dorms, proximity to classes, and social atmosphere.

Off-Campus Housing

The Lowdown On...
Off-Campus Housing

Undergrads in Off-Campus Housing:
Freshman 30%
Others 82%

Average Rent For:
1 BR Apt.:
West Campus: range from $470-$1200, most around $750

North Campus: range from $400-$900, most around $650

Riverside: range from $400-$600, most around $400

Other Areas: range from $375-$895, most around $550

2 BR Apt.:
West Campus: range from $600-$2000, most around $1700

North Campus: range from $600-$1600, most around $1250

Riverside: range from $400-600

Note: On Riverside, you pay per bedroom. Everyone is responsible for only their own rent.

Other Areas: range from $665-$1610, most around $1000

3 BR Apt.:

West Campus: range from $1600-$3600

North Campus: range from $1600-$2000

Riverside: range from $400-600

Other Areas: range from $964-$1925, most around $1300.

Best Time to Look for a Place:

October, when you want to secure a place the following August. Yes, it sounds crazy, but it is what you have to do if you want a good place around campus, especially in West Campus. If you are looking outside of West Campus, you can wait longer. If you are really brave and want to wait until the last minute, you can sometimes get a great deal by looking for an apartment in July or August right before you need an apartment in mid-August. But you never know what is going to be left over, so it is best to look early and get your lease signed.

Popular Areas:

North Campus
Riverside
West Campus

Leasing Offices to Call:

Avignon Realty
715 W. 23rd St
(512) 236-0002

Boardwalk Campus
Management
2417 Leon St.
(512) 499-0001

Ely Properties
608 West 24th Street
(512) 476-1976

Eyes of Texas Properties
409 W. 29th
512) 477-1163

Marquis Management
605 W. 28th
(512) 472-3816

Metro Realty
2401 Rio Grande
(512) 479-1300

Pioneer Property
Management
611 South Congress #510
(512) 447-4496

Tower Real Estate
2109-B Rio Grande
(512) 322-9934

Popular Complexes:

(more of a partying atmosphere)

900 West 23rd
24th and Pearl

Boardwalk on 24th
24th and Leon

Boardwalk on Leon
24th and Leon

(Popular Complexes, continued):

Boardwalk on Salado
Salado between 26th / 27th

Centennial
26th and Nueces

Croix
24th and Pearl

Crossing Place
Riverside and Crossing Place

Gables Central Park
38th and Lamar

Old Villas
25th and San Gabriel

Melrose
Riverside and Crossing Place

New New Villas
Villas Guadalupe
27th and Guadalupe

New Villas/Villas Nueces
22nd and Nueces

Old Main
25th and Pearl

Old San Gabriel
19th and San Gabriel

Orangetree
25th and Rio Grande

St. Thomas
25th and Pearl

Waterford
24th and Leon

Quieter Complexes:

21st and Rio Grande

(Quieter Complexes, continued):

Appletree
45th and Avenue A

The Georgian
22nd ½ and San Gabriel

Seton
25th and Seton

Stoneleigh
25th and Leon

University Gardens
22nd and Rio Grande

Other Complexes to Look At:

Cornerstone
24th and Rio Grande

College Park-The Landings
4700 E. Riverside

Jefferson Commons at
the Ballpark
4600 Elmont Dr.

Lenox
23rd and San Gabriel

Robbins Place
21st and Robbins

Sabinal
Graham and San Gabriel

San Gabriel Square
23rd and San Gabriel

Stones Throw
Nueces between 24th and 23rd

Valencia
Graham and San Gabriel

(Other Complexes, continued):

Vanderbilt
22nd and San Gabriel

Villa Vallarta
25th and Longview

The Village at Riverside
Riverside and Crossing Place

Westridge
26th and San Gabrie

For Assistance Contact:

Austin Apartment Association

www.austinaptassoc.com

(512) 323-0990

info@austinaptassoc.com

Students Speak Out On...
Off-Campus Housing

"Stay near campus. Riverside is cheap but kind of ghetto towared the East side, so if you can afford to live closer, do so. West campus is fun and close to the fraternity parties, so you can just walk over."

Q "Housing is becoming more convenient as the market is becoming flooded. **It remains expensive around the campus area, but finding a place is not a problem**. The areas off campus that house mostly students offer the best amenities for the least amount of money, while on-campus locations offer better convenience, and more of a college feel."

Q "It's pretty easy to find a place off campus after your first year. There are tons of realtors who will help you find a place nearby campus. However, beware—most **management places for West Campus properties suck, and they always try to screw you out of your money** and rights as a renter. Always threaten with calling the Texas Apartment Association."

Q "I liked living in my dorm, and I would have stayed there had there not been **a stigma on people who lived in the dorm after one or two years**. Off campus is nice for those who are more mature and don't mind driving. But if you live in West Campus, you can walk anywhere fairly easily."

Q "**Off-campus housing is plentiful, but a bit overpriced**. If you're looking for a deal, wait until the last minute, or go to Riverside which is South Austin, East of I-35. The UT shuttle runs throughout many apartment complexes out there."

Q "I would tell everyone to live at Waterford because it used to be the most fun party apartment in West Campus, but unfortunately, it was bought by Campus and Central Properties and they have ruined the place. Now, I would strongly advise against living there or any other apartments that they manage, because they definitely suck the life out of fun apartment living. Live elsewhere if you don't want to get screwed over, and you do want to have fun in your apartment building. **Some good choices are the Villas properties, the Boardwalk properties, Centennial, Old San Gabriel, and Orangetree**. I don't know much about 900 W. 23rd, but you might check them out, too; they are new, so they should be nice. Croix, St. Thomas, and Old Main are okay. I would personally never live on Riverside, but the apartments there are really nice if you are willing to live that far away from campus. Or look into houses in West Campus as there are some nice ones."

Q "I lived in a Campus and Central Properties-owned apartment building, and I would not wish that torture on anyone. **They were hard to contact when you had a problem**. The elevator was working but not turned on the entire time I lived there, and they were unresponsive to requests to fix it or turn it on. They were also very uncooperative at move-out, after a long list of other problems. Most people who live in any of the Villas properties seem to like where they live, but you have to lease very early to get a space. You must choose roommates and sign a lease no later than October or November if you want a prime West Campus apartment."

Q "West Campus is pretty expensive because it's so close to everything. However, **you can find many equally nice places farther away, and then just take the bus**. UT students can ride all Metro buses for free with their student ID."

Q "Housing off campus is convenient, but pricier if you want to live within walking distance. Sometimes **you run into problems with realtors and apartment management companies**, such as Campus and Central Properties."

Q "I lived in West campus the last three years of college. It was so convenient. Unfortunately, **if you want to find a good place, you have to start looking before New Year's**. Go to *www.taa.org* to check out Management before you rent. Ely Properties managed my first two places, and they tried to screw us out of our deposit. If your management tells you anything that sounds funny, check with TAA or one of the Law professors to see if it's true. Also, if you ask to be present during the final inspection, they have to arrange a time so you can be there . . . it's the law, no matter what they say. I lived in University Gardens last year, and the management was great and prompt."

Q "There are a lot of places in West campus that are nice, but they tend to be expensive. There are many other places in Austin to live, but **you risk living around hippies and weirdos if you move north** . . . wait, there are hippies and weirdos everywhere."

The College Prowler Take On...
Off-Campus Housing

I definitely recommend the dorm experience for your freshman year, but after that, it is time for something new and time to live on your own. That's right, it's time to get an apartment and have to cook for yourself, clean for yourself, pay bills, as well as have parties and invite members of the opposite sex over as often as you want. Yeah, having an apartment is great. If you want to live near campus and you don't mind paying a premium, West Campus is the place to be, especially if you are Greek, as this is where the sorority and fraternity houses are located. However, if you are not Greek, or Greek-oriented, don't turn your nose up. There are plenty of non-Greeks in West Campus too, as it is the best and most convenient place to live while at UTA. To clarify, West Campus is not actually on campus, but it is to the west of campus across the Drag.

The apartments in West Campus vary from new and nice, to old and trashed, but nearly all are highly priced. This is because of their convenience to campus, and you almost never get everything you pay for. However, they are easily within walking distance to school. If you want to be lazy or it's raining, there is the West Campus Shuttle Bus. When dealing with campus area apartment management companies just be aware that some companies try to take advantage of college students. If something doesn't sound fair or right, it's probably not. Some companies are known for taking students' deposits, so if you feel you have been treated unfairly, talk to the company. Go over what they used your deposit for and make them explain it to you. If they are still taking advantage, call the Texas Apartment Association or a lawyer, and don't be afraid to get your parents involved.

Riverside is another heavily populated student area that is much lower priced, and you get a lot more amenities for what you pay for. The apartments on Riverside generally have nice pools and health clubs, basketball and volleyball courts, and are inexpensive enough for students to have their own rooms. The only downside is that you have to ride the bus drive to campus, and it is almost impossible to find a place to park. The other downside is that Riverside has a somewhat higher crime rate than other areas of Austin, and everyone has to be more careful when they are in that area.

North Campus is another popular area, and most apartments there are as expensive as West Campus, but there are some less expensive choices, as well. There are many options around Austin on the UT shuttle routes, so you can find housing that is much less expensive than the housing found nearest to campus. Unfortunately, you won't have the convenience of walking to school, and parking on campus is never an easy task.

The College Prowler® Grade on

Off-Campus
Housing: B

A high grade in Off-Campus Housing indicates that apartments are of high quality, close to campus, affordable, and easy to secure.

Diversity

The Lowdown On...
Diversity

Native Indian:
0%

White:
61%

Asian American:
17%

International:
3%

African American:
4%

Out-of-State:
5%

Hispanic:
15%

Political Activity

Very high on the UT campus. Austin is a very liberal town and UT is a very liberal campus. However, the conservatives also have their voice. One of the biggest controversies on campus every year comes from a conservative group, Justice for All, an anti-abortion group. And on the liberal side, Guadalupe was shut down from MLK to Dean Keeton for six hours in spring of 2003 during an anti-war protest.

Gay Pride

Austin is pretty cool, and it's definitely the liberal bubble of Texas, so the gay acceptance is probably higher here than anywhere else in Texas. There are gay organizations on campus such as She Says, Lesbian, Bisexual, and Gay Students Association, Rainbow Summit, OUTlaw, MBA OUTsource, and even an all-gay fraternity, the Delta Lambda Phi Colony. But again, there are definitely the more conservative students on campus who may not be as open-minded. Over all, UT is pretty tolerant.

Most Popular Religions

Christianity is pretty popular on campus. There are several churches on campus, and you will often see people on campus passing out bibles or preaching. This is in addition to the many Christian groups that can be found on campus. There are alot of Jewish students at UT, with Hillel just across the street and several organizations on campus. The Church of Scientology is one you can't miss, as it is huge and directly across from campus, so if that interests you, they are always recruiting. Many students are non-religious, or at least, they do not go to church regularly while at school here. But if you are looking for some religion, check out the booths on the West Mall, ask friends in the dorm where they go to church, attend Greek bible studies, or just look around campus or in the phone book. You can try a different church every weekend for months.

Economic Status

There are definitely all levels of economic status here at UT. It depends on where you look as to what kind of impression you get about the economic status here. There are wealthy students, students from middle-class families, and students with very little money. With 50,000 students, there are obviously going to be great disparities in the economic status of the students here. Some students are completely funded by financial aid, while others pay their way by working their way through college, and then there are students completely funded by their parents.

Minority Clubs

Black Health Professions Organization, Beta Alpha Psi, Thurgood Marshall Legal Society, Society of Hispanic Professional Engineers, Multicultural Awareness Society, Longhorn College Chapter of the N.A.A.C.P., S.E.E.D. (Society Encouraging Excellence through Diversity), Minority Culture Committee, Minority Women Pursuing Law, Student Recruitment and Orientation Committee, Asian American Relations Group, Queer People of Color, Jewish MBA Association, Indian Graduate Business Association, Asian Pacific American Coalition, Longhorn American Indian Council, Hindu Students Council, Latin American Linguists and Anthropologists, Indian Cultural Association, Mexican Student Association, Hillel Jewish Students Association

Did You Know?

Students represent all 254 counties in Texas, all 50 states and 115 foreign countries.

Students Speak Out On...
Diversity

"The campus is very diverse, which sometimes can be an annoying thing to deal with. Everything seems to be controversial, and it sometimes makes things uncomfortable for all."

Q "The campus, since it is so large, has **a very bad self-segregation problem**. The sororities and fraternities are basically all white. If you want to associate yourself with only your race, it is very easy. The diversity numbers for UT, particularly with respect to African Americans, is pathetic, but I do not see a large-scale improvement happening due to serious racial tension in the community."

Q "It's a little too diverse for me. But of course, **I'm a redneck from the backest of backwoods**, so it seems that way anywhere I go!"

Q "It's so diverse that all the groups generally tend to keep to themselves. **It's not uncommon to hear conversations in Spanish, German, Japanese, or Korean** while riding the bus or walking across campus."

Q "It depends on whom you ask. **The numbers are horrible**. It also depends on whom you hang out with and where you live. You have to get involved in organizations and go to special places if you want to see anything other than white people. But they are there, you just have to find them."

Q "This is a very liberal campus. **Not everyone is white and Republican in Austin**. There is plenty of ethnicity."

Q "We don't have that many African Americans, but we have more Hispanics and Asians, and I believe that may be because of the ethnic makeup of our state. I'm not sure what the exact numbers on our state are, but I do know that **there are more Hispanics than African Americans in Texas**, so it would make sense that they outnumber the African Americans at the University of Texas. There is a majority of whites in Texas, so there is a majority of whites at the University of Texas. I just wish everyone would chill out."

Q "**Everyone's WASP or Asian**."

Q "The campus is very diverse. But I don't like that **the state legislators are trying to force diversity upon us**."

Q "UT is extremely diverse. There are young adults from countries all over the world. **There are people here from Timbuktu to Lake Titicaca**. The diversity was at first unfamiliar to me, but then I realized what a great experience it is to interact with people from different backgrounds."

Q "The **administration makes diversity an issue**. If you've ever seen the movie PCU, UT is trying to do the same thing."

Q "**The push for diversity seems to be creating a more segregated campus**. The recruitment of minorities is unnecessary and counterproductive. They force difference in race down our throats, while trying to convince us that we're one big happy family."

The College Prowler Take On...
Diversity

Diversity on the UT campus is a rather touchy subject. Our school is predominantly white (61%). However, there are definitely minorities on campus, and they often make themselves known. Many students feel that our student body is too diverse, and depending on where you are on campus, it can definitely seem as if the minorities are the majority on campus. The Hopwood case in 1997 banned Affirmative Action at the University after white students sued the UT Law School when African American students who were less qualified were let in, and the white students were not. The "Top 10 Percent Rule" was implemented to take the place of Affirmative Action post-Hopwood, though it really has not done much for minority enrollment.

There is not a lot of tension between minority and majority groups on campus. Many minority groups tend to keep to themselves on campus. Some groups on campus, Student Government being one of them, want to force a mandatory diversity class on all students. This will not likely help relations on campus, and has resulted in a number of heated debate in the campus newspaper, the *Daily Texan*, for months. It seems at times that the Administration caters too much to minority groups on campus. There are special groups on campus that focus on increasing minority enrollment and starting programs to get students from high schools that are not typically represented at UTA. There are several majors dealing with African American studies, Asian American Studies, Mexican American Studies, and Middle Eastern Studies. So, if one positive, minority students who do get accepted into UTA certainly won't find a biased course catalog.

B+

The College Prowler® Grade on

Diversity: B+

A high grade in Diversity indicates that ethnic minorities and international students have a notable presence on campus and that students of different economic backgrounds, religious beliefs, and sexual preferences are well-represented.

Guys & Girls

The Lowdown On...
Guys & Girls

Men Undergrads:	**Women Undergrads:**
48%	52%

Birth Control Available?
Yes, University Health Center-SSB

Most Prevalent STDs on Campus
Chlamydia

Social Scene

The social scene on and around the UT campus is definitely one of the most positive things about this university. We are often ranked as one of the top 10 (or at least in the top 20) party schools in the nation. The students at Texas definitely know how to have fun. Whether it is storming Guadalupe after Ricky Williams won the Heisman, and thousands of students were singing the "Eyes of Texas," while others climbed on top of a Capital Metro Bus, or a rowdy frat party, the social scene at UT can't be beat. After we win a home football game, there are always huge celebrations on campus, at the fraternity houses, and downtown. Organizations on campus have house and apartment parties, and this is a great way to spend time with your friends outside of working on the main purpose of your organization, whether it be political, service, honorary, or social.

Hookups or Relationships?

The people who want to be in relationships, at least the guys, are in them. Most guys want hookups (not to say that girls don't want them, as well), but it is pretty much guaranteed that guys are interested in casual hookups. Freshman year is definitely not a time for relationships, as there are too many people to meet to be tied down. I also don't recommend long distance relationships or relationships where one partner is still in high school during your freshman year. This is especially true if you will be living in a coed dorm. Cheating will occur. I've seen it too many times, and as much as you want to say you won't do it, it is more than likely going to happen. So, you might as well just go to college single and be able to do what you want to do without hurting someone else. Dating, as in going out on dates, is almost non-existent here, outside of relationships. Dating consists of hanging out, going to parties, or maybe going to or meeting up at a bar. I would ask the new generation of Longhorn men to try and change this, and take the girls out on real dates once in awhile. Trust me, they'll appreciate it.

Best Place to Meet Guys/Girls

With 50,000 students on campus and 7,000 freshman in your class, there have got to be a few that you like. A great way to meet people is if you live in a coed dorm because everyone is right there, either right down the hall, next door, or on the next floor. And the coed dorm is also very conducive to hookups, as everyone is located quite conveniently. Fraternity parties are also a popular place to meet people, and alcohol helps everyone overcome any shyness they might possess. Students might also meet someone in class—a novel idea. Study groups are good for your grade point average, as well as your social life, if you pick those you find most attractive to join your group. Bars, once you are 21, are definitely a place to meet people, and you could meet a different sort of person than the type you normally hang around with. Sixth Street attracts people from all over Austin, not just students. Organizations on campus are another opportunity to meet people, and these people you know you will have something in common with.

Did You Know?

Top Three Places to Find Hotties:

1. Fraternity parties
2. Downtown
3. Dorms

Top Five Places to Hook Up:

1. Frat houses
2. Bars
3. Dorms
4. Mt. Bonnell
5. Your bed, you exhibitionist you

Dress Code

You can wear anything at UTA when you are going to class. It's easy to spot the freshmen girls on campus because they are the ones who take the time to shower before class, to put on full makeup, to wear a skirt and cute top. Once girls get older, they realize that it doesn't matter what they look like for class and they wear what everyone else wears: T-shirts, jeans, pajama pants, soft shorts, wind pants, sweat shirts, tank tops, little or no makeup, un-showered. You can tell the freshmen guys by the orange shirts that they wear to class at least three days a week. A little thing we like to say is, "We get it, you got in!" Once they grow out of that, guys wear T-shirts, jeans, khaki shorts, athletic shorts, wind pants, khaki pants, sweatshirts, and polo shirts. Pretty much everyone in the Greek system will wear their Greek T-shirts almost everyday on campus. Flip-flops are definitely a must on campus, and they are worn year-round, as it never really gets too cold for them. Reefs are very popular, as are Rainbows. Lots of guys wear boots, New Balance tennis shoes, and Merrells are also pretty popular.

Students Speak Out On...
Guys & Girls

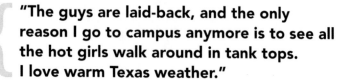

"The guys are laid-back, and the only reason I go to campus anymore is to see all the hot girls walk around in tank tops. I love warm Texas weather."

Q "**I can't remember the last time I was walking around UT and didn't see a hot guy**. They are everywhere. With about 25,000 men running around, you are bound to find a cute one! Many days, I am overwhelmed with the hotness around me in my classes, but that usually means I'll go, so that helps me out."

Q "The girls are the hottest in Texas. **All my friends that attend other universities and come to visit me simply gawk whenever they are on campus**. It doesn't get any . better. Your odds aren't too bad, either, with approximately 25,000 college-aged women within walking distance. You can't strike out every time."

Q "I love the southern gentlemen at this school. The guys who are polite and who were raised right are so awesome, so **thank you, moms, for raising your sons properly**. The guys who go out in cowboy hats and wear boots are so hot, and if they drive a truck that is even sexier! If you become a Silver Spur, you automatically become a girl magnet—probably because of the boots and hat. The baseball team is full of cute guys, and their games are never as crowded as they should be, considering all the cute guys, and how well the team has done in the past few years. If 80,000+ fans can show up for our football games, a few more of us should show up for the baseball team."

Q "Think we're usually ranked in the **top five or ten schools with the most attractive people**."

Q "It depends on where you look. There are a lot of cute boys, athletes, and some frat boys, plus everywhere else on campus. **There are also not-so-attractive people**. It just depends on what you're interested in."

Q "They are incredible! **There is every kind of girl you could ever want to meet here**. We have one of the best-looking student bodies of any university I've ever visited."

Q "**UT girls were just voted the hottest in the country** by *Playboy*'s first actual college poll, not the fake ones that always get passed around."

Q "Guys here are not my pick for the good-looking group and **the girls here dress up way too much for going to class**. Many of them are spoiled and take a lot for granted."

Q "**The guys on the crew club team and the volleyball club team are especially cute**. Also, there are always cute guys in the business school. Studying at the law library is always a good idea to try and pick up cute older guys. And I happen to know some very hot Pikes, so girls, definitely go to their parties if you want to find some cute, nice, laid-back guys. As for girls, I personally think sorority girls are definitely a good choice. Overall, we are a highly attractive group, and we know how to have fun. However, stay away from any girls who will only drink Zima or wine Coolers. If they can't learn to drink beer or at least mixed drinks, they are going to be way too high-maintenance, and you don't need to put up with that hassle. Trust me, I am very old (23) and wise."

Q "There's no stereotype for the girls. There are **all different kinds and sizes**, and they're pretty hot."

Q **"I've lived in seven states, and Texas guys are the best**. I actually dated a guy at West Point, but he was from Texas and UT was his second choice. Usually, all us girls are pretty tan due to the great weather. Texas joins other southern states in their reputation for politeness and hospitality, so people down here are genuinely nice for the most part."

The College Prowler Take On...
Guys & Girls

Texas, overall, is an attractive state and UTA, the largest university in the state, is certainly no exception. *Playboy* has repeatedly named the girls at UT some of the hottest in the nation, and the guys aren't too bad either. There are every type of guy and girl on this campus. With 50,000 students how could you not find someone that you find attractive? Styles here range from skater to sorority girl, hippie to prep, activist to stoner, model to "anything but," frat boy to thug, prissy girl to outdoorsy and, of course, there's a fair share of nerds and jocks. You can find whatever it is you are looking for at UTA. However, it is somewhat difficult to find someone who wants the same things that you want, i.e. a relationship or no strings attached, depending on your philosophy and your current place in life.

The guys at UT agree that the girls here are hot and they enjoy going to class for the eye candy, if nothing else. The guys here unfortunately have yet to win any awards, but there are definitely a lot of good looking ones out there. This campus may not be as diverse racially as other campuses, but there is definitely a diversity in the types of people at this school. So, whatever your type is, you should be able to find someone who suits your fancy.

The College Prowler® Grade on
Guys: A

A high grade for Guys indicates that the male population on campus is attractive, smart, friendly, and engaging, and that the school has a decent ratio of guys to girls.

The College Prowler® Grade on
Girls: A+

A high grade for Girls not only implies that the women on campus are attractive, smart, friendly, and engaging, but also that there is a fair ratio of girls to guys.

Athletics

The Lowdown On...
Athletics

Athletic Division:
NCAA Division I

Conference:
Big 12, Football I-A

School Mascot:
Bevo the Longhorn

**Males Playing
Varsity Sports:**
288 (2%)

**Females Playing
Varsity Sports:**
262 (1%)

Men's Varsity Sports:
Baseball
Basketball
Cross-Country
Football
Golf
Swimming & Diving
Tennis
Track and Field (indoor)
Track and Field (outdoor)

Women's Varsity Sports:
Basketball
Cross-Country
Golf
Soccer
Softball
Swimming & Diving
Tennis
Track and Field (indoor)
Track and Field (outdoor)
Volleyball
Rowing

Intramurals:
Flag Football
Soccer
Volleyball
3-on-3 Basketball
Kickball
5-on-5 Basketball
Tennis
Badminton
Racquetball
Table Tennis

(Intramurals, continued)
Billiards
Golf
Swim Meet
3 Sport Challenge
Turkey Trot
Bench press

Club Sports:
(www.utrecsports.org)
Aikido
Archery
Badminton
Ballet Folklorico
Ballroom Dance
Baseball
Crew
Cycling
Dance Team
Equestrian
Fencing
Field Hockey
Gymnastics
Handball
Ice Hockey
Japan Karate
Judo
Kendo
Lacrosse (mens's and women's)
Marathon Team
Polo
Power Lifting
Racquetball
Roller Hockey
Rugby

(Club Sports, continued)
Sailing Club
Sailing Team
Men's Soccer
Women's Soccer
Squash
Tae Kwon Do (ITF and WTF)
Tennis

Ultimate Frisbee (men's and women's)
Volleyball (men's and women's)
Water Polo (men's and women's)
Water Ski Team
Wushu

Getting Tickets

Sports Package - students can order the Longhorn All-Sports Package with their registration for only $70. This makes students eligible for the draw for tickets for all home games for all UT sports. It is a great investment, as regular tickets for every game would greatly exceed the $70 cost. However, student season tickets are really the more important investment because you are guaranteed the same seats for every game, you don't have to go through the draw, you can make a block with your friends, and you can get a ticket for the OU and for the A&M games. This is definitely the way to go. However, if you are not an upperclassman, don't expect to get the best seats.

Most Popular Sports

Definitely football, basketball, baseball

Overlooked Teams

Swimming & diving, volleyball, rowing

Best Place to Take a Walk

South Mall, Pease Park-West of Campus, near Lamar Blvd., the indoor track in Gregory Gym, from campus to the Capital Building, up and down the Drag

Fields/Facilities

Dr. Nasser Al-Rashid Strength Complex

Penick Allison tennis center (capacity 1,000)

Bellmont Hall

Clark field

Disch-Falk Field (capacity 6,649)

Frank Erwin Special Events Center (capacity 16,175)

Gregory climbing wall

Gregory Gymnasium (capacity 4,400)

Gregory pool

Anna Hiss Gym

Indoor practice facility

Stadium at Joe Jamail Field (capacity 80,106)

Lee and Joe Jamail Texas Swimming Center (capacity 2,600)

Red and Charline McCombs Field (capacity 1,252)

Mike A. Myers Stadium and Soccer Field (capacity 20,000)

IPRC Commons Rec Center

Recreational Sports Center

Darrell K. Royal Memorial Texas Rowing Center

Whitaker fields

Whitaker tennis courts

Did You Know?

While Ricky Williams was playing for Texas, many people called him "little Earl" because his awesome playing style was reminiscent of another UT running back, Earl Campbell. While Earl Campbell was playing football at Texas he was awarded the Heisman Trophy, and is the only Longhorn to have won the O'Brien Memorial Trophy for the outstanding player in the southwest.

Ricky Williams was not only awarded the Heisman Trophy in 1998, but he also won the **Doak Walker award for the best college running back in both 1997 and 1998**. Also in 1998, he received the Maxwell award, which honors the nation's outstanding college football player. Ricky is also the only University of Texas player to win The Walter Camp Football Foundation Player of the Year trophy, which is awarded to the nation's top player who has exemplified the qualities of self-discipline, unselfish team play, desire to excel, mature judgement and respected leadership.

➡

The Longhorns also have **two winners of the Lombardi Trophy**, Tony Degrate in 1984, and Kenneth Sims in 1981. Tommy Nobis, like Ricky Williams, was awarded the Maxwell award in 1965. Three Longhorns have also won the Outland Trophy—Scott Appleton in 1963, Tommy Nobis in 1965, and Brad Shearer in 1977.

Fourteen Longhorns can be found in the **National Football Hall of Fame**.

The Texas Longhorns have **won a total of 43 national championship titles**.

The men's swimming and diving team were **back-to-back national champions** in 2000, 2001, and 2002.

Did You Know?

Women's track and field, both indoor and outdoor, won **two back-to-back national championships** in 1998 and 1999.

Texas Longhorns have won **47 gold medals**, 25 silver medals, and 10 bronze medals at the Olympic Games

The **University's first football game was played in 1893**. The first Texas-Texas A&M game was played in 1894.

The University of Texas has **won more Big 12 titles** in men's and women's sports than any other school.

The University of Texas has produced **42 olympic medalists.**

In the **fall of 2002,** *Sports Illustrated* named UT number 1 among the nation's 324 Division I athletic programs.

Current and former Longhorns won **21 medals at the 2004 summer Olympic Games** including 11 gold medals.

Students Speak Out On...
Athletics

> "Varsity sports are huge! We support our teams by coming early, being loud, and staying late . . . and wearing burnt orange. IM sports are also very big. It's a great way to stay in shape and have fun with your friends."

Q "**Varsity sports are very big on campus**. Lots of people participate in IM sports."

Q "If you come to Texas and you don't know about Texas football, then you came to the wrong school and should just turn around and go back to that cave you crawled out of. Texas football madness never ends in Austin. **When the season ends, we start talking about next season**. Football season is the most fun time of year, as you can feel the energy in the air on campus. Alums come in on buses, by car, by plane, and by limo. They have box seats, season tickets, and lifetime passes. They've been coming here for 30 to 50 years, they used to play here, and Darrell Royal was probably their coach. We have players who are third-generation Longhorn football players, like the legendary Koy family from Bellville. Texas football is awesome. Go to the games, yell loud, be with your friends and enjoy a magical experience. And when you are an alum and get season tickets, come back and support your school. Bring your kids back to experience what you experienced, and hope that they want to continue your tradition and become Longhorns, too."

Q "Varsity sports are huge, and they **keep getting bigger each year**. The IM sports program is huge, and students are often very involved."

Q "Varsity sports? What varsity sports? Oh—the sports that got UT named #1 sport school by *Sports Illustrated* last year. **Get a sports package when you register for classes**. Then, fill out the application with your friends for football season tickets, and always buy extra OU and A&M tickets—if you don't use them, you can sell them for a few hundred dollars on eBay. If you get season tickets, you don't have to wait in line for days to attempt to draw tickets. IM sports are for everyone, from the suckiest player to the near walk-on. They're organized by skill level, which means everyone can play!"

Q "Almost every club participates in IM sports teams. I play IM volleyball, basketball, and softball every year. **They have competitive divisions, too**. Varsity sports are big here; enough said."

Q "**Get season tickets for football** so you won't have to wait in the draw line."

Q "**IM sports are awesome**, football is king of varsity sports, the others all get second billing."

Q "Can you say football? I don't know many other universities that have **F-16 flybys at their football games**. Basketball would definitely come in second in terms of fun for fans. We're good at lots of sports, but who wants to watch golf or swimming?"

Q "Varsity and IM sports are huge. **This is Texas, after all**."

Q "The school is so big that all sports, IM and varsity, are big. **There's always something to do**."

Q "Hook 'em Horns! **IM sports are highly competitive** and actively participated in."

The College Prowler Take On...
Athletics

If you come to Texas apathetic about sports, you are 1) crazy, and 2) missing out on some great games, fine athletes, and fun times. Buy a sports package; it gives you the opportunity to draw for tickets for all of the major varsity sports games. Football at Texas is huge, even when we are not ranked, though this has not been the case for several years. Basketball fans are almost as rowdy and, in 2003, both men's and women's basketball made it to the Final 4. Our baseball team doesn't gather as many fans as it should considering we won the College World Series in 2002 and regularly make it to Omaha for the final tournament. However, the boys at Disch-Falk do have their loyal following.

Especially under-appreciated are the swimming and diving teams who are often Big 12 champs, but never get the recognition that they deserve, aside from a lighting of the Tower orange every year. Women's rowing has also grown a lot in the past few years, and their team generally does pretty well. They also do not get the credit that they deserve. Intramurals are very popular within the Greek community, dorm communities, and campus organizations. Texas also has many club teams that do very well, including men's rowing, men's volleyball, and watersking. If you have time, you should check out one of the club team tournaments in addition to all of our varsity teams' games.

The College Prowler® Grade on
Athletics: A

A high grade in Athletics indicates that students have school spirit, that sports programs are respected, that games are well-attended, and that intramurals are a prominent part of student life.

Nightlife

The Lowdown On...
Nightlife

Club and Bar Prowler: Popular Nightlife Spots!

Club Crawler:

311

311 E. 6th St., between Trinity and San Jacinto

(512) 477-1630

311 is a Blues Club, very laid-back, not your typical blaring techno music dance club. It is a very fratty scene, but there are definitely all types. There are the bikers, hippies, Texas Exes, and businessmen.

(311, continued)

311 attracts all ages, there are very often older men and women dancing with college kids or up on stage with the band. It is a very intimate setting, very enjoyable, and open till 2:00 a.m.

→

Element

301 W. 5th St., 5th and Lavaca

(512) 480-9888

Thursday through Saturday, it's open till 3:00 a.m. Thursday is Latin Night and Friday is Ladies Night. This club plays hip hop and R&B and hass 13,000 square feet of space for partying for the crazy club kids of Austin. There are even three full bars to top it off. However, they do have a dress code to uphold—no shorts, sandals or tennis shoes. So dress up in your finest and visit this Warehouse District hot spot.

Emo's

603 Red River, 6th and
Red River

(512) 477-3667

Emo's is the place to be if you are punk, trying to be, or are just into the music. They are one of the few places downtown that will let those poor, neglected minors in, so head on down there—all ages, all the time. They definitely get some pretty good bands down there, like Ash, Jimmy Eat World, and Saves the Day, so if you're into that scene, check it out.

KAOs

2003 E. Riverside

(512) 445-6888

KAOs is a club on Riverside, where one of the DJs from the Beat 104.3 broadcasts from on the weekends. To describe the club, I will take a quote from *austin.citysearch.com*, a personal review from someone who has visited the club: "Kaoz iz tight, it be comin real. I just don't like it when they play techno. It might be ghetto but aint nothin' wrong with that. I still have a good time with all my homies at Kaoz!!"
So, if that is your kind of place, you know where to go.

Paradox

311 E. 5th St., 5th and Trinity

(512) 468-7615

Paradox is always 18 and up, and doors open at 9 p.m. Friday's Mega 93.3/99/7 is at Paradox with DJ Jason Tolfa for Hip-Hop, R&B, dance hall and reggae broadcast live on 93.3/99.7. Saturday's Mega 93.3/99.7 is back live at Paradox handing out free stuff.

Platinum X

419 E. 6th St.

(512) 476-7088

Plays every type of music from dance and trance, to hip hop and R&B. Platinum X has four bars and three dance floors, and it's always 18 and up. As it is 18 and up, this tends to be a rather young crowd, many taking advantage of the fact that they can get in here underage, so if you're older and just want to dance, I don't recommend this for you. However, if you are a guy looking to get with young girls, you are in the right place. Just make sure she's out of high school, please.

Roxy

304 E. 6th St.

(512) 477-7523

Roxy is another popular 6th Street dance club for the scantily clad girls and randy young men. It's ot an upscale crowd by any means, and they definitely tend toward the younger side of 21. These party animals dance like it's spring break, especially on Thursday College Nights.

Spiro's

611 Red River St., 6th and Red River

(512) 472-4272

Spiro's has gone through some changes over the past few years, and it was recently bought and renovated. Spiro's now has five bars and three dance floors, including an outdoor back patio area/dance floor that is very nice. The main dance floor plays everything from '80s and '90s dance and pop songs to techno music. The second dance floor has hip hop, R&B, and rap, and there is a VIP lounge. The club's most popular dance floor is its Latin Patio, hosting live bands and DJs playing salsa, Spanish rock, and current Latin dance music. Tuesday is Salsa Night outside on the back patio, and a dance instructor gives free lessons at the club from 8:30 p.m. to 10 p.m.

Texture

505 Neches, 5th and Neches

(512) 480-8921

Texture claims "Austin's best dance vibe." The Texture story is a "Celebration of self-expression, all preferences, all colors: Texture celebrates who we are as individuals, no matter of what race, color, creed, or choice. Texture will embody creativity by combining light, color, language, music and movement to shape ideas and visions." If that sounds interesting to you—check it out. It closes at 4 a.m.

Bar Prowler:

Aquarium on 6th

403 E. 6th St., 6th and Trinity

(512) 499-8003

http://aquariumbar.com

This is usually a very crowded bar filled with college students. It's a place where you will likely run into someone that you know. There's no cover, and you get a free T-shirt on your birthday.

Hours: Tuesday-Sunday
8 p.m.-2 a.m.

Cain and Abel's

2313 Rio Grande,
West Campus

(512) 476-3201

This is the place to be on Tuesday nights when you live in West Campus. You can walk there, and therefore walk home. You can drink $1 beers from 7 p.m. to 11 p.m. This is a very popular Greek hangout. They also now serve food all day and until 5 a.m.

Minors can get in during the day and after 2 a.m.

Hours: Monday-Friday
4 p.m.-2 a.m., Saturday-Sunday
8 p.m.-2 a.m.

Cheers Shot Bar

416 E. 6th, 6th and between Trinity and Neches

(512) 499-0093

On the weekends, it gets pretty crowded, and the main bar is narrow, so it can be hard to get around. However, during the week, it is usually not very crowded. There is also an upstairs and a small downstairs, as well as a back patio that can get you away from the crowd. This is more of a place to go get a shot or two and then move on, rather than sitting and hanging out. They have lots of fun shots to try.

Hours: Open daily from
9 p.m.-2 a.m.

Fadó Irish Pub

214 W. 4th St, 4th St.

(512) 457-0172

www.fadoirishpub.com

Fadó is a little bit of an older crowd since it is on 4th St., but the college crowd still hangs out there. It is usually crowded and very dark, covering a broad range of traditional, contemporary, and progressive Irish and European music. Get a Guinness, Boddingtons, Harp or Bass on tap. Fadó provides live satellite feeds for Gaelic games, rugby, and English premiere league soccer, to name just a few.

Hours: Open daily from
11:45 a.m.-2 a.m.

Happy hour food specials from $2.95. Specials change weekly.

Ginger Man

304 W. 4th St, 4th St.

(512) 473-8801

www.gingermanpub.com

Ginger Man is a beer bar located on 4th Street that is pretty cool. It's best to be unpretentious in its pretentious 4th Street surroundings. There are 80 beers on tap, and more than 100 bottled beers to choose from, so for the connoisseur of Coors, this is the place. They also have a good wine and cider list. Overall, it's not a bad place to check out, very chill, usually pretty crowded, but not to the point that you can't move without stepping on someone.

Hours: Monday-Friday 2 p.m.-2 a.m., Saturday-Sunday 1 p.m.-2 a.m.

Iron Cactus

606 Trinity, 6th and Trinity

(512) 472-9240

www.ironcactus.com

This is both a restaurant and a bar serving mostly Mexican food, some seafood dishes, and a few other interesting dishes thrown in, such as duck quesadillas. There is an upstairs patio where you can sit outside and look out over 6th Street. It is a very nice view, romantic and relaxing. In the winter there are heaters, and in the summer, there are misters, so you are comfortable throughtout the year.

(Iron Cactus, continued)

I recommend the Limorita-it is pink, and is made with Bacardi Limon and tastes like pink lemonade. Try the Cactus Juice, which has Everclear in it.

Bar Hours:
Monday-Wednesday 1 p.m.-12 a.m., Thursday-Friday 11 a.m.-2 a.m. Saturday 12 a.m.-2 a.m.

Kitchen Hours:
Monday-Friday 11 a.m.-11 p.m. Saturday 12 a.m.-11 p.m., Sunday 4-10:30 p.m.

The Library

407 E. 6th, 6th and Trinity

(512) 236-0662

www.librarybars.com/austin

Usually a very crowded bar filled with college students. The Library and Aquarium are pretty similar bars, and are right next door to each other. You often go from one to the other. If you can find somewhere to sit, it's a good, chill bar.

Hours: Sunday 8 p.m.-2 a.m. Monday-Tuesday 7 p.m.-2 a.m. Wednesday-Friday 4 p.m.-2 a.m., Saturday 7 p.m.-2 a.m.

Logan's
200 E. 6th, 6th and San Jacinto
(512) 236-0300

Plays lots of good '70s, '80s, and '90s music (all songs that you know and can sing to). It has a small dance floor where there are always people dancing.
Hours: Monday-Friday 4 p.m.-2 a.m., Saturday-Sunday 11 a.m.-2 a.m.

Other Places to Check Out:

Agave
415 E 6th St.
(512) 469-7892
Hours: Sunday-Wednesday 8 p.m.-2 a.m., Thursday-Saturday 8 p.m.-2 a.m.

Blind Pig Pub
317 E 6th St
(512) 472-0809
http://www.blindpigpub.com
Free barbeque every Longhorn away game!

Buffalo Billiards
201 E 6th St.
(512) 479-7665
www.buffalobilliards.com/austin

Chuggin' Monkey
219 E. 6th St.
(512) 476-5015
www.thechugginmonkey.com
Open 7 days a week from 8 p.m.-2 a.m.

Dizzy Rooster
306 E. 6th St
(512) 236-1667
www.thedizzyrooster.com

Fuel
607 Trinity St.
(512) 472-8557
www.spillonsixth.com/fuel
Open nightly 9 p.m.-2 a.m.

Maggie Mae's
www.maggiemaesaustin.com
Go upstairs on the patio—it is beautiful, and one of the most chill places to hang out on 6th St. Great weekly drink specials, and a free cover coupon on their Web site.

SoHo Lounge
217 E 6th St.
(512) 472-1916

Great martinis, great shots, fun dance floor

Spill
212 E 6th St.
(512) 320-8005
http://www.spillonsixth.com

Treasure Island
413 East 6th St.
(512) 476-4466

$2.00 Test tube shots every night! There's never a cover except Sunday night, and it's 21 and over.

The Vibe
508 East 6th St.
(512) 474-0632
www.liveatthevibe.com
Club hours: 7 days a week 7 p.m.-2 a.m

Coffeehouses:

JP's Java
2803 San Jacinto
(512) 494-0015
Hours: Monday-Friday
6 a.m.-2 a.m., Saturday-
Sunday 6 a.m.-12 a.m.

Little City
2604 Guadalupe
(512) 476-2326
www.littlecity.com
Hours: Monday-Friday
7 a.m.-12 a.m.

The Metro
2222 Guadalupe
(512) 474-5730
Open 24 hours

Mojo's
2714 Guadalupe
(512) 477-6656
www.mojosdailygrind.com

Mozart's Coffee Roasters
3826 Lake Austin Blvd.
(512) 477-2900
www.mozartscoffee.com
Hours: Monday-Thursday
7 a.m.-12 a.m., Friday 7 a.m.-
1 a.m., Saturday-Sunday
8 a.m.-1 a.m.

(Coffeehouses, continued)

Spider House
2908 Fruth
(512) 480-9562
www.spiderhousecafe.com
Saturday-Sunday
8 a.m.-12 a.m.

Starbucks
504 W. 24th St.
(512) 472-5211
Hours: Monday-Friday
6 a.m.-11:30 p.m., Saturday-
Sunday 6:30 a.m.-11:30 p.m.

Cool Places to See Music:

311
Antone's
Austin Music Hall
The Back Room
The Backyard
The Continental Club
Emo's
Gruene Hall
La Zona Rosa
Stubb's
The Vibe

Bars Close At:
2 a.m.

Cheapest Place to Get a Drink:
The Library and Aquarium

Favorite Drinking Games:

Kings

Beer Pong

Card games

Power Hour

Student Favorites:
Aquarium, the Library, Logan's, Cheers Shot Bar, Cain and Abel's, and Fuel

Useful Resources for Nightlife:
www.austin.citysearch.com
www.austin360.com

Primary Areas with Nightlife:
6th Street - College Crowd
4th Street - Slightly Older Crowd
Campus Area - Students
Red River - Music Scene

Local Specialties:
Texas Beers: Lone Star, Pearl, Shiner Bock, Ziegenbock,

Frats:
See the Greek Section!

Students Speak Out On...
Nightlife

"Everything is fun around here. Sometimes parties might seem more cliquish than some other universities, but it may just be because we're one of the largest universities in the country."

Q "Let's start with 6th Street. Since Austin can be rowdy, **there are really good drink specials at any given time**! Treasure Island has dollar drinks one weekday night that can put studying on the back burner very fast. Cain and Abel's is the cool place to go on Tuesdays because they have dollar bottles. It's always packed. I am partial to Trudy's—their Mexican Martinis are delicious and lethal. You're only allowed to have two, and that's all you need anyway."

Q "Sixth Street is always fun and has a college crowd, as well as a more mature older crowd. **I personally can't stand 4th Street because it is so pretentious**, and everyone thinks that they are so cool because they are out of school and in that young working professional age. I could not care less. Plus, there are never any drink specials, and you have to dress up. Sixth Street is just much more laid-back, and you always see people you know."

Q "Don't walk around carrying a drink. **Bars on 6th street blow unless it's your birthday**, and even then they're too crowded."

Q "**Apartment parties are everywhere**. It's hard not to feel the presence of the massive Greek parties, but if you don't go Greek, don't despair, you can still get together with 30 people or so around a keg."

Q "**There are no parties on campus**, but the equivalent will be the West Campus parties, which are all the same. It's a lot of white people getting drunk listening to the same kind of music. It can be fun, depending on who you're with and how drunk you are. There are tons of bars and clubs off campus. Go to 4th, 5th, 6th, or 7th Streets on any given night. Find something that seems like you'd like it, and just go in. The possibilities are endless."

Q "**Greek life is pretty big, the fraternity parties are fun**. Bars are stupid until you're 21, but then it's to Abel's near campus, and then to 6th street."

Q "If you're a guy, join a fraternity or make some friends in one so that you can have a place to party. **As for off campus goes, two words: Sixth Street**."

Q "Parties aren't allowed on campus, but there are festivals. However, in the immediate proximity of campus, **parties can get large, wet, and wild** . . . literally. Some of the fraternities throw parties titled Wet and Wild, Beach Bash, Bellyflop, Hurricane, Island, and there are lots of foam parties throughout the year. My favorite bars are the Library, Aquarium, and Ginger Man—they have so many different beers."

Q "There is always a party to go to. **The bars are great on your birthday** because you get a free shot at every bar!"

Q "**There are lots of bars on 6th street if you like being around Mexicans and meatheads**. There are other good places like Abel's near campus that have a better crowd."

Q "I have not been to too many parties on campus, but the bars and clubs offer a wide variety. **Good spots include Cain and Abel's and Katz's because of the good food**."

Q "UT hosts festivals on campus—one year they paid for Ludacris to give a free concert at the Tower. The tailgates before football games are right across the street from campus on MLK, and they can get rowdy! Sixth Street is more for the younger college crowd; **4th and 5th have a few gay bars/clubs and good bars for the 23+ crowd**. The Ginger Man, and Fado's Irish Pub have great beers. Hang out on the deck over the lake at Hula Hut and share a Hulala fishbowl punch; or take Pat Green's advice to hit up El Arroyo, literally over a ditch, and drink great margaritas. These places are great for after class or work, with great laid-back, outdoor atmospheres."

The College Prowler Take On...
Nightlife

Austin's nightlife is never boring. No matter your personality, you shouldn't have a problem finding something to do. From concerts to bars, country to punk, laid-back to rowdy, beer to martinis, 6th street is the place to be once you turn 21 or when you have a really good fake ID. Don't try to go downtown unless your ID is good, because you will get caught. Underage drinking violations are rampant. In recent years it was a lot easier to drink underage, but they have cracked down since then. If you are underage, there are always other options—coffeehouses, fraternity parties, dorm and apartment parties, and the like.

If you don't like the downtown scene, you can always hit the restaurant bars like Trudy's, Iron Cactus, Baby A's or the campus-area bars like Cain and Abel's. Whatever you like to do you can find it in Austin and at the University of Texas. The fraternity parties are always fun. Dorm parties are more common in the private dorms, but Jester is rumored to have some pretty fun floor parties. The popular apartment complexes on West Campus and Riverside frequently have parties, so if you want a quiet place to live, look into other neighborhoods or smaller complexes. Some places on 6th Street are certainly not for the faint of heart.

The College Prowler® Grade on

Nightlife: A

A high grade in Nightlife indicates that there are many bars and clubs in the area that are easily accessible and affordable. Other determining factors include the number of options for the under-21 crowd and the prevalence of house parties.

Greek Life

The Lowdown On...
Greek Life

Number of Fraternities:
27

Undergrad Men in Fraternities:
9%

Number of Sororities:
24

Undergrad Women in Sororities:
12%

Fraternities on Campus:

Acacia
Alpha Tau Omega
Beta Theta Pi
Chi Phi
Delta Chi
Delta Kappa Epsilon
Delta Sigma Phi
Delta Tau Delta
Delta Upsilon
Kappa Alpha
Kappa Sigma
Lambda Chi Alpha
Phi Delta Theta
Phi Gamma Delta
Phi Kappa Psi
Phi Kappa Theta
Pi Kappa Alpha
Pi Kappa Phi
Sigma Phi Epsilon
Sigma Alpha Epsilon
Sigma Alpha Mu
Sigma Chi
Sigma Nu
Sigma Pi
Theta Chi
Zeta Beta Tau
Zeta Psi

Sororities on Campus:

Alpha Chi Omega
Alpha Delta Pi
Alpha Phi
Alpha Epsilon Phi
Alpha Xi Delta

(Sororities, continued)

Delta Gamma
Delta Delta Delta
Chi Omega
Kappa Delta
Kappa Kappa Gamma
Kappa Alpha Theta
Pi Beta Phi
Sigma Delta Tau
Zeta Tau Alpha

Multicultural Greek Organizations:

Affiliate Groups: Gamma Beta, Sigma Lambda Delta,

Asian Fraternities: Omega Phi Gamma, Lambda Phi Epsilon

National Panhellenic (African American)

Sororities: Alpha Kappa Alpha, Delta Sigma Theta, Zeta Phi Beta

Fraternities: Kappa Alpha Psi, Omega Psi Phi

Texas Asian Panhellenic Council: Alpha Kappa Delta Phi, Kappa Phi Gamma, Sigma Phi Omega

United Greek Council (latino/a groups)

Sororities: Kappa Delta Chi, Sigma Lambda Gamma

Fraternities: Omega Delta Phi, Sigma Lambda Beta

Other Greek Organizations:

Gamma Sigma Alpha
Greek Council
Greek Peer Advisors

Interfraternity Council
Order of Omega
Panhellenic Council

Did You Know?

Fraternity and sorority members are **28 percent more likely to graduate** than their non-Greek peers.

Kevin Dunn from *The Real World: Back to New York* went to UT. He was in the communications school, and he was a member of Delta Tau Delta.

Matthew McConaughey was a Delta Tau at UT.

Farrah Fawcett was a Texas Tri Delt (Delta Delta Delta).

Kay Bailey Hutchison and Ima Hogg were members of Pi Beta Phi at the University of Texas.

Jim "Mattress Mac" McIngvale from Gallery Furniture in Houston, was a Pike (Pi Kappa Alpha) at UT, as was **Fess Parker who was Disney's Davy Crockett** in the 1950s.

Lynda Bird Johnson, LBJ's oldest daughter, was a Zeta (Zeta Tau Alpha) at Texas.

Pi Beta Phi was the first sorority on the UT Campus and will be 105 years old in 2007.

If a chapter's name is Texas Alpha, it means it was the first of its national organization to be founded in that state. Pi Beta Phi and Sigma Phi Epsilon are both the Texas **Alpha chapters at the Univeristy of Texas**.

Students Speak Out On...
Greek Life

"The Greeks get a bad rep around campus, but honestly it's the best way to go socially, as they have the best parties, and you can also make business ties for the future. Learn to play golf."

Q "**Being Greek is a great way to make the University seem smaller**. As a girl, the rush process is so rigorous that you bond with those around you, and when you pledge, you are suddenly united not only with those who wear your letters, but with all who wear letters, because we are a minority, and we stick together."

Q "Everyone seems to have an opinion about the Greek system here. **It is one of the more expensive organizations you will find**, and that might cause stereotypes to become more prominent. It seems like a good thing for some, and maybe a hindrance for others, depending on the reasons for being there and how much they branch out both inside and outside the organization."

Q "**In the white Greek system, life can be equally as fun or better without being Greek**. In the black Greek system, the social scene is dominated by the hard-to-enter Greek organizations. The Indian, Hispanic, and Asian Greek scenes fall in the middle of these two extremes."

Q "Greek life is big, but does not dominate campus like it does at smaller schools. **Only 21 percent of campus is Greek**."

Q "**The Greek system and its members are a somewhat persecuted minority**. The *Daily Texan* is constantly putting us down; everyone thinks that we are all racist, that we never do anything but party and drink, and that we don't do anything for the community. The truth is that as a group we do a ton for the community, and being in these organizations teaches us leadership roles, how to run meetings, deal with budgets, manage people, work with the community, and public relations. Yes, we do have parties, and yes, many people do drink, but that is not just the Greeks, that is college students in general."

Q "Greek life is strong at UT, but not as strong as other universities (i.e. Texas Tech). However, we, the Greeks, still like to have a lot of fun, and **we do have better parties than Tech**. There is also so much more to do in Austin than Greek life, so it doesn't dominate the social scene."

Q "I completely recommend joining a fraternity or sorority. It is a great experience that gives you many opportunities to meet people on campus, get involved in service projects, have somewhere to belong, and always have something social going on. **Greek organizations require their members to keep a certain GPA** or to participate in study hours, so it can be good for your academics, as well. Being in a sorority is something I would never change, and if I were a guy, I would have joined a fraternity without question because your social life increases exponentially."

Q "I'm Greek, and I wouldn't have it any other way. **I don't know what non-Greek people do on the weekends**, but I bet it's not as fun. There's always something going on during on the weekends, and during the week, for that matter."

Q "Greek life is okay. **It definitely doesn't dominate the social scene**. Most of the big parties are put on by fraternities, but there are thousands of other things to do."

The College Prowler Take On...
Greek Life

Greek Life is not the focal point of this University's social life. However, going Greek is definitely a worthwhile choice to make. About 10-15 percent of the UT population belongs to a fraternity or sorority, and there are plenty of other options to choose from. But if you do choose to pledge, there are many benefits. Being Greek gives students a wonderful opportunity to meet people. Being in a fraternity or sorority allows students to make bonds that they will have for life, and gives them a bond that they can pass on to and share with parents, grandparents, siblings, children, and grandchildren.

The Greek system also gives its members the opportunity to make great contacts that can help students both during and after college when looking for employment, as well as being a source for internships, references, and letters of recommendation. For the most part, Greeks stick up for each other and will help each other out, especially if they are from the same fraternity or sorority. However, just being Greek can give you an extra edge if whoever you are dealing with also cares about being Greek. The largest part of the Greek system is the Interfraternity Council and Panhellenic Council, which are the traditionally white fraternities and sororities. There are separate Greek councils for African American, Asian American and Latino fraternities and sororities, as well. As with most other facets at UT, there is something for everyone.

Being Greek is not a necessity, especially at UT. This is a huge campus with hundreds of organizations and clubs that one can become involved in, so the Greek system can be bypassed completely. However, it is an extremely fun experience that I would recommend for anyone who thinks that they would at all enjoy it. If you want to meet more members of the opposite sex, and a higher ratio of attractive members of the opposite sex, the Greek system is the place to be. If you want a place to belong, an automatic group of friends, and to always have something to do, then being in a fraternity or sorority is a great idea.

There are definitely people who do not fit into the Greek system, and while some people know this beforehand, others drop out once they have pledged. That is totally fine, there are so many other organizations on campus to fall back on. But if Greek life looks like fun to you, definitely rush, you won't regret it.

The College Prowler® Grade on

Greek Life: B+

A high grade in Greek Life indicates that sororities and fraternities are not only present, but also active on campus. Other determining factors include the variety of houses available and the respect the Greek community receives from the rest of the campus.

Drug Scene

The Lowdown On...
Drug Scene

Most Prevalent Drugs on Campus:
Alcohol, weed, Ritalin, Adderall, cocaine

Liquor-Related Referrals:
304

Liquor-Related Arrests:
58

Drug-Related Referrals
85

Drug-Related Arrests:
29

Drug Counseling Programs:
Confidential Telephone Counseling 24 hours a day/ 7 days a week/365 days a year
(512) 471-2255

Campus Alcohol and Drug Education Program
(512) 475-8252

Students Speak Out On...
Drug Scene

> "Drug problems here are mostly with alcohol, and the interesting thing here is that people don't know that drinking every weekend can turn into alcoholism."

Q "There are drugs everywhere. Pot smoking is common, like anywhere else. Since it is in a city, **there is probably more access to drugs**, but I don't think it's any different than any other big city school."

Q "**There is a lot of pot and X**. A lot of alcohol and tobacco is used."

Q "It totally depends on who you are around. **You will probably know people who sell and use drugs from your dorm or apartment building**, and you may or may not be friends with them depending on your preferences. But, even if you are around drugs, people at UT are not into peer pressure—this isn't high school. You could go through your entire college career without ever seeing anyone using drugs depending on who you hang out with and where you spend your time."

Q "I have no experience with drugs, but **I'm sure I could find something if I wanted it**."

Q "**The use of marijuana is prevalent**, but I'm not too familiar with the use of harder drugs."

Q "It's there, but **I wouldn't say the campus has a problem with serious drugs**."

Q "There are **too many freaking drugs**."

Q "It depends on your friends. If you surround yourself with anti-drug users, you'll never see them. There are other people with whom you'll see drugs all of the time depending on where you party. By drugs, I mean things other than marijuana and alcohol—**everyone I know at this school drinks and/or smokes pot** . . . a lot."

Q "Everyone smokes pot, it is Austin after all. Cannabis and related products are widely used and accepted. **A lot of coke use goes on**, and 'shrooms are in supply."

Q "**Marijuana is common here**. I don't know about other drugs. If my extermination-of-hippies plan were put into force, we would have no drug problem."

Q "**This campus is fairly good about drug awareness**, but if people want something, they will find a way."

Q "Austin's still stuck in the '60s and '70s, so there's lots of marijuana. **Nobody has ever pressured me into using or buying drugs** because nobody really cares."

The College Prowler Take On...
Drug Scene

The most prevalent drugs on the UT campus are, without a doubt, alcohol and marijuana. However, if someone wants any type of drug, it is likely that he or she will be able to get it fairly easily. Most anyone knows someone, or knows someone who knows someone, who can get their hands on cocaine or any type of pill that they want—ecstasy, speed and the like. Heroin, however, does not seem to be that prevalent. Most students at UT drink, no matter what their age, and getting a hold of alcohol if you are underage is fairly simple.

Most students at UT consider weed not to be an illegal drug, but put it in the same category with alcohol. Whether you are a pot smoker or not, you will not feel pressure to do so at UT. Students here respect one another and tend not to violate another students personal space. So overall, drugs are available if you want them.

B-

The College Prowler® Grade on

Drug Scene: B-

A good grade means that drugs are not a highly-visible threat on campus. The poorer the grade, the more prominent the drug scene.

Campus Strictness

The Lowdown On...
Campus Strictness

What Are You Most Likely to Get Caught Doing on Campus?

- Getting a parking ticket—there is hardly anywhere where it is safe to park, unless you have a campus parking tag, and even then you have to be careful.

- Smoking weed in your dorm room

- Getting caught with alcohol underage

- TABC [Texas Alcohol Beverage Commission] likes to bust apartment parties around campus, especially if you are in a courtyard, where the alcohol is not completely contained in the apartment. They will likely be undercover, so be on the lookout for anyone who looks like they don't belong at your party, or who looks like they are in their 30s at a fraternity party.

Students Speak Out On...
Campus Strictness

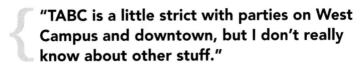

"TABC is a little strict with parties on West Campus and downtown, but I don't really know about other stuff."

Q "I have never had a run-in with Campus cops, although I think my friend passed out on the UT campus sidewalk on his 21st birthday party, and **they let him go with a warning right before he puked on the officer's shoes**. I think they are probably pretty lax."

Q "The security on campus seems kind of like a day-to-day thing. **Sometimes things can be overly strict and other times seem overly lenient**."

Q "**They are ridiculous about drinking**, and love to bust a minor, but other than that, they keep the place safe."

Q "I've **never really encountered Campus Police**."

Q "**They don't bring out the drug dogs**, but if you put it in their face and ask if they want a hit, they might react."

Q "**Tons of people do things on campus, yet not many get caught**. Be careful on 6th street, though, and be careful at parties because cops will arrest underage drinkers. If you are arrested on 6th street, you automatically spend a night in jail; no questions asked."

Q "**Drinking depends on how mean your RA is**. Drugs seem to be not tolerated on campus."

Q "**People drank every night of the week in my dorm**. The cops came once to bust a crazy party on another floor, and THEY told us that as long as we're in our rooms with the doors closed, they won't do anything."

Q "Both Campus Police and APD are realistic about the fact that they won't ever be able to stop the drug and alcohol use. **You have to be pretty wasted and belligerent to get busted for anything**."

Q "How strict are they? **Not very**."

The College Prowler Take On...
Campus Strictness

It is not a good idea to drink or do drugs openly on campus, or at least not outside. Drinking is technically not allowed in dorms on campus, nor are drugs allowed in private dorms (alcohol is allowed in some private dorms), but students definitely both drink and do drugs in their dorm rooms. Generally, though, the police are only called if the RAs decide to call them.

At the football games, be sure not to carry alcohol in your purse or in your boots, because many students are searched and patted down. Many people get drunk prior to the football game at a tailgate party or house party, and then they just arrive at the game drunk. The thing that UT is known to be most strict about is parking, and UTPD loves to write parking tickets.

The College Prowler® Grade on

Campus Strictness: B+

A high Campus Strictness grade implies an overall lenient atmosphere; police and RAs are fairly tolerant, and the administration's rules are flexible.

Parking

The Lowdown On...
Parking

UT Parking Services:
1815 Trinity St.
Trinity Garage, Room 1.200
(512) 471-PARK

Student Parking Lot?
Yes

Freshman Allowed to Park?
Yes, with a parking permit

Approximate Parking Permit Cost:
$50-$616

Common Parking Tickets:
Expired Meter: $15

Handicapped Zone: $100

Fire Lane: $50

Parking without an authorized valid permit: $25

Parking in an At-All-Times space requiring a specific permit: $50

Unauthorized parking in a State vehicle or University vehicle space: $20

Possession, counterfeiting, altering of parking permit and or possession of lost or stolen permit: $150 (plus the cost of the permit)

Did You Know?

Best Places to Find a Parking Spot
Brazos Garage, 27th St. Garage

Good Luck Getting a Parking Spot Here
Everywhere! There are 70,000 students, faculty, and staff at UT, and only 14,000 parking spaces, so good luck! This is why it is best to live at an apartment with parking at the building or an apartment close enough to campus so that you can walk to class. Your other option is living on a bus route so that you can take a bus to campus. Parking on campus is not your best option by any means.

Parking Permits

C - Any UT student "C" lots and "Any UT Permit" lots cost $89 annual

C+ - Any UT student "C" lots, "Any UT Permit" lots, and University garages cost $139 annual

R - Students living on campus: University garages (random selection draw for UT housing students) cost $616 fall and spring, $336 fall or spring, $225 summer

S - Commuting Students: University garages cost $510 annually, $240 Fall or Spring, $131 Summer

DC - Students with Disabilities: Any "D" parking space on campus for students with valid state of Texas disability placard or license plate cost $89 annually

Night Horn - Any UT student, faculty or staff: University garage, evening and weekend access costs $35 semester, $50 annually

Daily Paid Garage Parking - $3-$7

M - Any UT student: motorcycle parking, and "M" permit parking areas cost $50 annually

Students Speak Out On...
Parking

> "It's very hard to park on campus. Some of the private dorms sell parking spaces in their garages for the semester. Try Castilian, parking is across the street from campus."

Q "Parking on campus? Good luck—unless you play football. Somehow, **Ricky Williams always managed to find a place for his Hummer** when he was here. If you're going to the PCL after 5, you can park across the street in a lot next to Jester . . . but it's small."

Q "Parking is the ho of campus. **If you have a lot of money, you can get it**. If not, you're going to be looking all over town for a spot."

Q "**Getting a parking permit is the worst**. Game days are a variable mass of cars and people with no place to park in sight. I very rarely try to park on campus, unless I have 10 minutes to spend looking. There is a state lot which is free on nights and weekends on the south east side of MLK and Congress, which is where I park most of the time if I have to drive to campus. Oh yeah, the state parking lots have started to charge for parking on game days."

Q "**Parking sucks**. Don't even try."

Q "Don't try to park on campus ever. **It really is a nightmare**."

Q "**Parking on campus is a problem for most here**.
Campus parking convenience and availability would
receive an F from most."

Q "Most universities have bad parking situations. UT may be
the worst in the country (save NYU). **There's nowhere to
park unless you pay $7.00 a day to park in a garage**,
and you still have to trek through the Texas heat to get to
your class. Your best bet is to walk as a freshman. If you
live off campus, the buses are great!"

Q "**Always check for no parking signs**! If you don't, then
you'll be leaving here with a light wallet."

Q "Parking is horrible and expensive. You can live without
a car as a freshman, provided you aren't working far
from campus. **Everything you need is within
walking distance**."

Q "**Parking sucks** in all of UT and surrounding areas."

Q "Look for no parking signs, and check the signs for what
kind of permit you need to have to park in any given
space. You will get a ticket if you are lucky, you might get
the boot or towed if you are not. Towing isn't as likely on
campus, but around campus **you are guaranteed to get
towed at least once in your tenure at UT**. I've gotten
towed three times and taken friends to pick up their cars
numerous times, the most recent time being just this week.
Parking everywhere sucks, and I wish you luck."

Q "**Parking in Austin makes you want to cry**. Finding a
parking spot here is like finding gold."

The College Prowler Take On...
Parking

One universal truth at the University of Texas is that parking sucks! I really don't even recommend buying an on-campus parking permit if you can avoid it. The number of students more than triples the number of parking spaces available on campus, and that does not even factor in the faculty and staff. One way that you can get around the parking nightmare is if you have a motorcycle, as a motorcycle permit is relatively inexpensive, and there is almost always a place on campus to park your bike. Really don't try to park on campus without a permit. The guards will not even let you drive on campus unless you have a UT permit until after 5:45 p.m. So unless you can sneak around them, you don't even have the opportunity to look around for a nonexistent parking space to get a ticket in.

If you live near campus, you are in luck—most apartments come with parking spaces. But if you have several roommates, know that most apartments come with one parking space per bedroom. The parking situation is not only horrible on campus, but is also horrible in all areas surrounding campus, such as West Campus. So if you don't have a spot at your apartment, it is not the easiest task to find one everyday. The best ways to avoid the parking hassles are to walk to class, bike to class, or take one of the many buses that travel all over Austin and to the University.

The College Prowler® Grade on

Parking: D

A high grade in this section indicates that parking is both available and affordable, and that parking enforcement isn't overly severe.

Transportation

The Lowdown On...
Transportation

Ways to Get Around Town:

On Campus
T Shuttle Routes
(512) 474-1200
shuttle@www.utexas.edu

www.utexas.edu/parking

Shuttle Routes: Burton Drive (BD), Crossing Place (CP), Cameron Road (CR), Disch Falk (DF), Far West (FW), 40 Acres (FA), Intramural Fields (IF), Lake Austin (LA), Lake Shore (LS), Pickle Research Campus (PRC), Red River (RR), West Campus (WC), Wickersham Lane (WL)

Public Transportation
Capital Metro
(512) 474-1200

Taxi Cabs
American Yellow
(512) 452-9999

Roy's
(512) 482-0175

Austin Cab
(512) 478-2222

Ace Taxi
(512) 244-1133

→

Car Rentals

Advantage
local: (512) 388-3377

Alamo
local: (512) 530-3522
national: (800) 327-9633
www.alamo.com

Avis
local: (512) 530-3522
national: (800) 831-2847
www.avis.com

Budget
local: (512) 530-3350;
national: (800) 527-0700
www.budget.com

Capps Van and Car Rental
(512) 323-0003

Dollar
local: (512) 530-2278
national: (800) 800-4000
www.dollar.com

Enterprise
local: (512) 320-5850
(512) 453-4402
national: (800) 736-8222
www.enterprise.com

Hertz
local: (512) 457-1583
national: (800) 654-3131
www.hertz.com

Longhorn Car Rental
(512) 452-1773

National
local: (512) 530-3539
national: (800) 227-7368
www.nationalcar.com

Thrifty
local: (512) 530-6811
www.thrifty.com

Best Ways to Get Around Town

Have your own car

Walk

Bike

Take a cab

Capital Metro

Ways to Get Out of Town:

Airlines Serving Austin

American Airlines
(800) 433-7300
www.americanairlines.com

America West
(800) 235-9292

Continental
(800) 523-3273
www.continental.com

Delta
(800) 221-1212
www.delta-air.com

Frontier Airlines
(800) 432-1359

Funjet Charters

Mexicana Airlines
(800) 531-7921

Northwest
(800) 225-2525
www.nwa.com

Southwest
(800) 435-9792
www.southwest.com

United
(800) 241-6522
www.united.com

→

Airports
Austin Bergstrom
International Airport

(512) 530-ABIA

3600 Presidential Blvd.
Austin, Texas

Department of Aviation
Austin Bergstrom
International Airport

3600 Presidential Blvd.,
Suite 411
Austin, TX 78719

E-mail: airportinfo@ci.austin.
tx.us

Non-Stop Service to
Atlanta, Baltimore/
Washington (BWI), Chicago
(O'Hare), Cincinatti
(International), Cancun,
Cleveland, Dallas/Fort
Worth (Dallas/Love Field),
Denver, Detroit (DTW), El
Paso, Harlingen, Houston
(Bush Intercontinental),
Houston (Hobby), Las
Vegas (International), Los
Angeles, Lubbock, Memphis,
Mexico City, Midland/
Odessa, Minneapolis/St.
Paul, Nashville, New York/
Newark, Orlando, Phoenix
(International),
St. Louis (International),
Salt Lake City, San Diego,
San Jose, Tampa

How to Get to the Airport
Take I-35 South to Riverside
Drive, exit Riverside, go east
on Riverside to Highway 71
follow 71 until you see signs
for the airport and then take
the ABIA exit.

(How to Get to the Airport continued)
Take I-35 South to Ben
White/Highway 71, exit
there go east on Ben
White/Highway 71, and
follow 71 until you see
signs for the airport, and
take the ABIA exit

Take Airport Blvd South to
Highway 71, go East on 71
until you hit the ABIA exit

A cab ride to the airport
costs, from campus area,
around $20.

Greyhound
Austin Ticket Center
916 E. Koenig Ln.
Austin, TX 78751
(800) 229-9424

Amtrak
Texas Eagle
(800) USA-RAIL

Austin Station
250 N. Lamar Blvd.
Austin, TX 78703

Travel Agents
University Beach Club
(512) 469-0999

STA Travel
(512) 472-2900

API Travel Consultants
(512) 476-6764

Fun Ventures Incorporated
(512) 391-0212

Students Speak Out On...
Transportation

> "The bus system can get you a lot of places, and a UT student ID allows you to ride it for free all the time. Having a car is not a necessity, but of course, it is more convenient."

Q "I don't really have a comparison to anywhere, but I do know that **the city buses can take a very long time due to traffic** and system size."

Q "The buses are clutch . . . **it beats the hell out of walking**."

Q "Never used it, always walked. **Cabs from campus area to 6th cost about seven bucks**, and you always have a fun and interesting driver."

Q "**The buses are free to UT students**, so that's a plus, and it makes living off campus much easier."

Q "Very easy. **The UT shuttle goes all over town** to areas of high concentration of college kids, plus you can use the Austin bus system, too."

Q "It's convenient but scary. **You are risking your life on UT buses**. I was riding the bus once, and the bus driver pulled over to Burger King, stopped the bus, and ran inside. Everyone on the bus was just sitting there looking at each other. A few times at the bus stop by my apartment, the bus just drove right by us . . . oops."

Q "**I often use the bus**. There are many routes, but not enough of the most popular ones like Forty Acres and West Campus."

The College Prowler Take On...
Transportation

Transportation is one of the things that Austin and the UT campus do pretty well. Students can ride the UT shuttle buses as well as Capital Metro routes free with their Student IDs. There are several cab companies in Austin and they are easy to reach by phone. They are generally very fast when you call them except for their peak times. Peak times for cabs are Thursday, Friday and Saturday nights to go downtown. At those times, there is a longer wait, and there are many people fighting over the same cabs downtown trying to leave bars at 2:00 a.m. When you are trying to get downtown or leave downtown, call a cab early to minimize your waiting time.

The E-Bus is also a great option if the cabs are taking too long, and it is free. However, it only runs from 6th Street to West Campus and to Riverside. The downside to the UT shuttle buses are that you can sometimes wait for a long time for a bus, and if you don't leave in enough time for your class, you could be late. This is particularly true with the West Campus bus, if you don't time it just right, it could have been faster just to walk to class. The first time I rode a UT bus, I had a scary experience, I ended up across I-35 by the baseball field, and the bus driver just stopped and got out, and we sat there for 10 minutes. They tend to randomly do this, so if you're brave, ride the bus, but if you're not, walk.

The College Prowler® Grade on

Transportation: B+

A high grade for Transportation indicates that campus buses, public buses, cabs, and rental cars are readily-available and affordable. Other determining factors include proximity to an airport and the necessity of transportation.

Weather

The Lowdown On...
Weather

Average Precipitation:

Fall: 3.43 in. per month,
            66% humidity

Winter: 1.71 in. per month,
            67% humidity

Spring: 2.56 in. per month,
            68% humidity

Summer: 2.04 in. per month,
            64% humidity

Average Temperature:

Fall: 59 to 81 °F
Winter: 39 to 60 °F
Spring: 65 to 85 °F
Summer: 74 to 95 °F

Students Speak Out On...
Weather

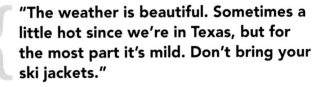

"The weather is beautiful. Sometimes a little hot since we're in Texas, but for the most part it's mild. Don't bring your ski jackets."

Q "Weather fluctuates wildly. **Yesterday, it was 80 and sunny. Today it's 40**. Bring all kinds of clothing."

Q "This is Texas; dress for anything. **We've had snow followed by a heat wave**. Summer is hot! Don't worry about dressing up for class. The first half of the semester, everyone sweats so much walking to class that dressing up makes you look stupid, not pretty."

Q "It's Texas; **your uneducated guess will be as good as the meteorologists'**."

Q "The weather is warm in August and September, perfect in October and November, then **basically, you'll freeze your butt off until March**."

Q "I love the weather here because it never gets too cold. And the best thing about the weather is it is always changing, especially in spring, winter and fall. It could be 85 degrees one day, and then it's down to 50 the next. It's great because if you're ever wanting a change, you will get it. Even in the summer, though it is in the 90s and 100s almost everyday, **there are those days where we have rain showers and thunderstorms**, and it will go down into the 80s or 70s. Then, it's just awesome outside, and you don't start sweating as soon as you walk outside. If you come to Austin, just be prepared for anything, and that includes the weather."

Q "Texas is hot. Austin isn't as hot as Houston, but **I wouldn't bring long underwear unless you're going skiing for spring break**. It's never a bad idea to have a sweatshirt in your bag even in the heat because the classrooms can be freezing. Find several pairs of comfortable jeans, you can wear them for at least a week without washing them."

Q "**It's warm more than nine months of the year, and you can wear flip flops almost year round**. Stay for at least one Austin summer in your college career. It's a great place to be if you like water—there are lakes and rivers close."

Q "The weather is **beautiful, warm, and sunny**! You must have khaki shorts and Reef sandals in order to survive."

Q "It gets really cold about a month out of the year and really hot the rest of the year. Otherwise, **there are about three weeks of fall and a week of spring**."

Q "**Hot**. Need I say more?"

Q "We have beautiful weather! It's warm and sunny. **You must have shorts and Reef sandals**."

Q "I hate the weather here. You would hardly know it is winter in Austin, and **I don't think it is a good idea to bundle up for 65 degree weather just to be fashionable**."

Q "The weather is pretty unpredictable. **I'd love to be a weather forecaster here, you can be wrong constantly and not get fired**. It'll be 80 degrees one day and 45 the next. The spring here is so beautiful—the sky is that impossible blue."

The College Prowler Take On...
Weather

The weather in Austin is unpredictable. You can have just about any kind of weather that you could want in Austin. It rains, it snows (every once in awhile). It's hot, it's cold, it's warm, it's cool, it's sunny and it's cloudy. And we average 300 days of sunshine a year. Could you ask for much more? We have summer/springtime weather nine months out of the year, fall for two months and one month of winter. It hardly ever gets really cold, and the winters are generally mild. It did snow in 2003, though, and that was fun for everyone— we even got a snow day off from school. However, this is definitely a rare occurrence. The summers are hot, with lots of days in the high 90s and 100s.

As for clothes, bring jeans and T-shirts, shorts and tank tops, sweatshirts and one jacket, but nothing too heavy because you will not need it. Oh, and don't forget your umbrella. It rains fairly often here, but it then clears up pretty clearly. A popular saying in Texas is "If you don't like the weather, wait 10 minutes." That saying definitely applies in Austin. Overall, the weather is great; just don't get too attached to any certain kind of weather, because it will change for sure.

The College Prowler® Grade on

Weather: B-

A high Weather grade designates that temperatures are mild and rarely reach extremes, that the campus tends to be sunny rather than rainy, and that weather is fairly consistent rather than unpredictable.

Report Card Summary

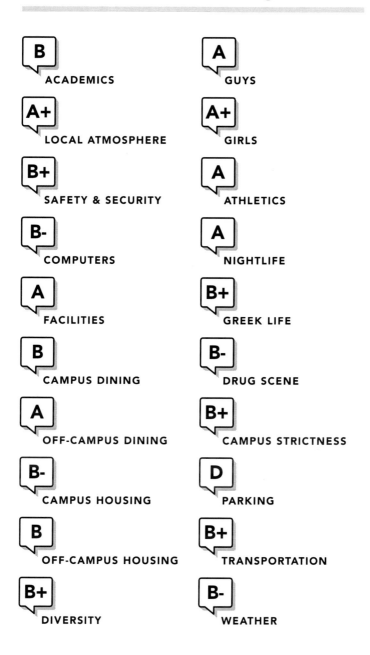

B ACADEMICS

A+ LOCAL ATMOSPHERE

B+ SAFETY & SECURITY

B- COMPUTERS

A FACILITIES

B CAMPUS DINING

A OFF-CAMPUS DINING

B- CAMPUS HOUSING

B OFF-CAMPUS HOUSING

B+ DIVERSITY

A GUYS

A+ GIRLS

A ATHLETICS

A NIGHTLIFE

B+ GREEK LIFE

B- DRUG SCENE

B+ CAMPUS STRICTNESS

D PARKING

B+ TRANSPORTATION

B- WEATHER

Overall Experience

Students Speak Out On...
Overall Experience

"I've gone back and forth with this question so many times, but I've learned more here than I could have anywhere else, and I'm a more mature and a better person for it all."

Q "I love it. I'm from Austin, and I could never leave. I love it too much. It's a good school on a pretty campus. **What more could a student ask for**?"

Q "I have wanted to be here since I can remember and never considered anywhere else. **The faculty is good, but the staff and advising departments leave much to be desired**, as they are often unorganized. The advisors seem to often be uninformed or not interested in going the least bit out of their way. I am sure there are many exceptions to this, but I have found very few."

Q "My overall experience so far has been great. **I don't wish I was anywhere else**."

Q "I love UT; it is the perfect place for me. I was going to go to the northeast to a small liberal arts college in Maine (Bates College), but **I thank the Lord everyday that I am blessed to still live in Texas**. I can't imagine myself happy anywhere else."

Q "**I wish I would have joined a club or organization**. Other than that, I loved it."

Q "I would not want to be anywhere else. I have loved my experiences at UT, both as an undergrad and **now in law school**."

Q "I am happy with my overall experience, and **I don't wish I had gone anywhere else**."

Q "Both of my parents went to school here, so **I have been a Longhorn fan my whole life**. Once I got to school here, it was obvious why my parents loved it here so much. I have had more fun here than I ever expected to have in college, and I never want to leave."

Q "I could **not imagine myself at any other school**."

The College Prowler Take On...
Overall Experience

Most students agree that they have loved their time here at UT, and they wouldn't want to be anywhere else. College is the best time of your life, and I can't think of a better place to spend it than at the University of Texas. Students get a great education while having an awesome college town with everything at their disposals. My advice: don't try to graduate early. In the words of Adam Sandler: "Stay in school, stay as long as you can . . . . For the love of God, cherish it!" Enjoy your time at UT—go cheer on the Longhorns at all the home games for all sports: football, basketball, baseball, intermurals. See the amenities that the Forty Acres has to offer—the Harry Ransom Center, go to our libraries and see our more than eight million volumes. Go to Gregory Gym and the Rec Center—you have a free gym membership for four years or more—use it.

I came to UT convinced that I was going to transfer to a school in California in the spring. I spent two days here before school started and I never wanted to leave, even to go home and visit my parents and high school friends! I couldn't leave because I was always afraid that I would miss something because there was always something exciting going on. If you are worried about the fact that UT is so big, don't. All you have to do is find your niche, and everything else should fall into place. You can find it within your dorm, apartment, organization, fraternity, sorority, or classmates. Although, at times, it may seem overwhelming, UT is not nearly as big as it sounds. All you have to do is make friends, which you will, and the campus will seem infinitely smaller. Come join us!

The Inside Scoop

The Lowdown On...
The Inside Scoop

UT Slang:

Know the slang, know the school. The following is a list of things you really need to know before coming to UT. The more of these words you know, the better off you'll be.

2222 - Koenig Lane on the East Side of Mopac, this also becomes Hwy. 290 on the east side of I-35. This is north of Campus.

2244 - Bee Caves Rd. on the West Side of Mopac, this is South of Campus.

6 Pack - The six buildings, Batts, Mezes, Benedict, Calhoun, Rainey, Parlin, that are located on the South Mall. Mostly liberal arts classes are held there, so probably every freshman will have an intro class in one of these buildings.

6th or Downtown - 6th Street is where most of the college bars are, and when people are going out, this is probably where they are going.

Abel's - Cain and Abel's

➜

Amy's - Amy's Ice Cream, the closest location to campus is at 35th and Guadalupe. They have fun ice cream flavors like Shiner (like the beer), Belgian Oreo, Tuaca, Mexican Vanilla, Guinness, Trifle and then you can also get a crush'n like Butterfinger, Snickers, or strawberries. It is an Austin original.

Baby A's - Baby Acapulco's, a popular Mexican restaurant to get margaritas—better margaritas than food, but try it for yourself.

Big 12 - The athletic conference to which the University belongs. UT is a part of the southern division of the conference with Baylor University, Oklahoma State University, Texas A&M University, Texas Tech University and University of Oklahoma. Schools in the northern division include Kansas State University, University of Colorado, Iowa State University, University of Kansas, University of Missouri and University of Nebraska.

The Castle - Some people's nickname for Castilian.

Cedric - Cedric Benson

Chance - Chance Mock

The Co-op - The University Co-op on the Drag. This is where you buy your books, UT clothing, school supplies, and any other UT paraphernalia. There is also the Co-op for Women and the Co-op Annex with discounted clothing. Both are just a few doors down.

Daily Texan - The campus newspaper. It has a rather liberal point of view, so that is something to remember; however, it is good to read to keep up on campus events. The Firing Line is where people write in to complain, and that section is always entertaining.

Dean Keeton - Name of 26th Street while it is on campus

Dirty's - Dirty Martin's Kumbak Café on 27th and Guadalupe— great and cheap burgers

The Drag - Guadalupe Street- it borders UT and has stores and restaurants such as The University Co-op*, By George, Urban Outfitters, Chipotle, Texadelphia, Einstein Brother's Bagels.

The Co-op should not be confused with A co-op which is a place where some students live cooperatively in housing where they share housework and cooking.

Drag Rat - Homeless or just wandering people who look somewhat unwashed. They live, sit, sleep, play music or beg on the drag. Don't give them money. Don't feel guilty about having money in your pocket. You could sit on the sidewalk all day, too, and ask for handouts, but you are contributing to society by getting and education. Generally, they will just sit around and play with their dogs, and ask for your money. However, they might not be homeless at all, they may just be a strange guy who went to your high school and decided to pretend to be a drag rat.

Earl - Earl Campbell

East Mall - The mall east of the Tower. This is a route you can take when you walk to the Stadium, and the Geology building. The large East Mall fountain is located there. It is located on the East side of the Tower, farthest away from the Drag.

Forty Acres - The original UT campus was located on 40 acres surrounding what is now the Tower. This is the area framed by 24th, Speedway, 21st, and Guadalupe Streets.

GDI - Someone who is not in a fraternity or sorority, stands for God Damn Independent.

Gregory - Gregory Gym

Hardin House - Also known as the Virgin Vault and Hard-on House

Hooking Up - Messing around, fooling around, making out, but not necessarily having sex. It can be anything from kissing to "everything but." Typically when you actually have sex you say you actually had sex, so hooking up does not mean having sex, but the definition really varies from person to person.

Hyde Park - An area north of campus that many students choose to live, there are houses and apartments and the rent is often cheaper.

Jester Jail - Some people sometimes refer to Jester as this because of its resemblance to a prison

Mack - Mack Brown

Mexican Martini - Margarita served in a martini shaker and martini glass with olives.

Midnight Rope-a-Ho - Midnight Rodeo

MIP - Minor in Possession of Alcohol, lots of people get lots of these while in college, very commonly given downtown. If you have gotten into a bar with a fake ID and a cop comes in, definitely put down your drink before the cop sees you. If he checks your ID and sees it's fake and you don't have a drink, you might get out of a ticket . . . probably not, but it's worth a try. If you are at an apartment party with alcohol there and you are a minor, you are almost guaranteed an MIP whether you are drinking or not.

MLK Blvd - 19th Street

MoPac - Mopac and Loop 1 are the same. The freeway west of campus, MoPac stands for Missouri Pacific because of the rail line that runs parallel to it.

Natty - Natural Light Beer

Old Villas - The Villas on San Gabriel, these were the first built in 1998. New Villas or Villas Nueces are the Villas on Nueces. New New Villas or Villas Guadalupe are the Villas on Guadalupe. Simple, yes, but something to know.

OU - Two meanings: the school, University of Oklahoma, one of our biggest rivals, as in, OU Sucks!; Also, the weekend in October when we travel to Dallas to play OU at the Cotton Bowl. As in, "Who are you going to OU with?"

PI - Public Intoxication, another 'fun' ticket that TABC can give you, very often happens downtown. Try not to get into fights, don't stumble around, or to slap a police horse.

A Purple - A purple margarita at Baby A's, they are their strongest margarita.

"Q" Drop - A notation appearing on a student's transcript when they drop a class between the 12th class day and the 4th week of classes. This notation indicates a drop without an academic penalty. Approval must be given by the chair of the department offering the course and by the student's advisor and dean.

The Rec - Rec Center

Red River Shootout - the annual game in Dallas between Texas and OU played at the Cotton Bowl.

Renaissance Market - Area of the Drag at 23rd Street where locals and hippies sell their handmade-wares, jewelry, candles, purses, candle holders; also called Hippie Square.

Ricky - Ricky Williams

Riverside - A street, but also an area where many students live. There are many luxury apartment communities such as Melrose and Crossing Place which offer cheaper living for students, but not the convenience of apartments nearer to campus.

Roy - Roy Williams

Sco Pro - Scholastic Probation

Shacking - Spending the night over at someone's house/dorm/apartment (usually a member of the gender to which you are attracted to) with or without hooking up.

Sorostitute - A derogatory term for a girl who is in a sorority, implies promiscuity.

South Mall - the mall facing the Capital, where the 6 pack is located.

TABC - Texas Alcohol and Beverage Commission, the feared and evil cops who will give you an MIP or PI if you are caught drinking. They are always out on 6th Street, will try to get into frat parties, and will walk in undercover into apartment parties if the door is open, so keep the door closed and don't let people in that you don't know, especially if they look like they're 30+.

Tex - The voice on the line when you use the phone to register for your classes. This is almost obsolete now that most registration is done online. However, there is an icon for Tex that you can push on the webpage after you register to hear Tex's voice. Everyone should do it at least once. It is a Texas institution that is being phased out by technology, and that is very sad.

TJ - T.J. Ford

Town Lake - The same as a part of Lake Austin which is actually the Colorado River

West Campus - Not actually a part of campus. It is West of campus, and covers the area from roughly 19th to 29th, and Guadalupe to Lamar. Many UT students, though, consider WC a part of campus.

West Mall - The mall facing the Drag. There are often tables out with different organizations passing out flyers, recruiting members or volunteers.

Villas - The Villas are a popular place to live in West Campus, especially for sophomore sorority girls, so guys, you might want to get in there too. However, there are several Villas and you must know what to call each of them.

Vince - Vince Young

Y'all - You all, you guys.

Note: Some buildings are only referred to by their 3 letter nicknames, most others are called by their full names-such as Welch and Batts. Here is a listing of the buildings referred to by their nicknames and what they stand for.

ACES Building - Applied Computational Engineering and Sciences Building

CMA - Communications Building

CPE - Chemical and Petroleum Engineering Building

ECJ - Ernest Cockrell Jr. Hall

ESB - Experimental Science Building

NOA - North Office Building A (Yes, you can have classes there.)

PCL - The main library, Perry Castaneda Library

RLM - Robert Lee Moore Hall

SSB - Student Services Building (This one can go either way, some people call it SSB, some call it the Student Services Building, or the Health Center)

UGL - Undergraduate Library—ithe same building as the FAC-the Flawn Academic Center.

UTC - University Teaching Center, across from the Business School.

Things I Wish I Knew Before Coming to UT

- Keep up with your reading because it will come back to bite you in the a$$.

- Student season tickets are the way to go for football.

- If a street is named after a river, such as Rio Grande, Colorado, Leon, they run north and south. If a street is a numbered street, it runs east and west.

- If an address is 2323 San Antonio, that means it is located at 23rd and San Antonio; 2401 Leon means 24th and Leon.

- When your parents are coming in town for a visit, and if they don't know their way around, buy them a map. There is nothing worse than Parents Weekend with a bunch of lost parents going the wrong way on one-way streets.

- Don't go to the Health Center for a gynecological exam.

- You can get free condoms at the Health Center.

- Don't judge other people too quickly because they're figuring out what they think and who they are, just as you are. In two weeks you might be doing what you would have judged them for.

- Your ideas and beliefs about everything, i.e. getting drunk the night before a test, will change when you get to college. It doesn't mean that you are a bad person and it's okay, it happens to everyone.

Tips to Succeed at UT

- Go to your professor's office hours. It will help him know who you are, and will show that you are interested in learning and could help your grade at the end of the semester.

- Keep up with your reading in your classes, or you will regret it at exam time.

- Start meeting people as soon as you get to schoo—in your dorm, on campus, wherever. You will be glad you did.

(Tips to Succeed at UT, continued)

- If you are at all thinking about going to graduate school or working in the field that you are studying in, make friends with your teachers, and stay in contact with them throughout college. Just stop by their office hours, or send them an e-mail every once in awhile. You will need a letter of recommendation from them at some point.

- Try to block your classes close enough together so that you don't have a class in Jester and then one in the CMA the next hour. This is so that you don't have to make it all the way across campus in 10 minutes. That hike is killer. And unless you are a speed demon, you will be a little late to your second class, or you'll have to leave your first class a little early.

- Go to class. (Special circumstance if you can't understand your professor, there are notes on the web, you will not be penalized for not attending class, or you can use the time you should be in class for studying, then it is okay to skip class). But overall, going to class can really help your grades.

- Make friends in class who you can get notes from if you have to miss class.

- Get a flu shot.

- Meet your professors and TAs.

- Have study groups that are productive.

- Join some sort of organization.

- Block your classes together; you will be more likely to go.

- Pick a major that you are interested in, but don't be afraid to change it once you get here. If you don't like your classes, you will not do as well.

- Make friends with your advisor so that they know you and can help you. They may be able to get you into that class that you absolutely have to have but couldn't get into.

- Make friends with your dean if it is at all possible, as they may be able to write you a great letter of recommendation if you need it.

UT Urban Legends

- If a virgin ever graduates from UT, the horses in Littlefield Fountain will fly out of the fountain.

- If you see an albino squirrel on campus before you take a test you will get an A.

UT Traditions

The University colors, orange and white, were officially adopted by the Board of regents on May 10, 1900, after a student vote. As early as 1885, students had used orange and white ribbons on special occasions. Athletic teams later unofficially adopted burnt orange as their color of choice. This is a good choice, as that other UT (Tennessee) school is also orange and white, and we need to distinguish ourselves. The official colors, as used in the University seal, are focal orange and pure white. The second place colors were orange and maroon . . . wouldn't that have been interesting?

Big Bertha, the largest marching drum in the world, became the "Sweetheart of the Longhorn Band" in 1955. Big Bertha was originally built for the University of Chicago, but luckily for the University, Longhorn band lover and supporter, D. Harold Byrd, and the band director of the time, Moton M. Crockett, purchased and brought Big Bertha to her final home right here in Austin. When Bertha is brought out for football games, her handlers are known as the "Bertha Crew."

The UT school song was composed by John Lang Sinclair. It is considered by some a sort of unofficial state song, was first sung at a minstrel show to benefit the University track team at the Hancock Opera House in Austin on May 12, 1903.

The "Hook'em Horns" hand signal that is known across the nation and to Texas fans everywhere was introduced at a Friday night pep rally in Gregory Gym before the Texas Christian University football game in 1955. Harley Clark, head cheerleader, and his friend, Henry Pitts, invented the sign, which is made by extending the index and little fingers and tucking the middle and ring finger beneath the thumb. Harley thought this would be a great symbol for University of Texas students because it resembled the head of a Longhorn.

Smokey the Cannon creates the thunderous roar that is heard after each Longhorn touchdown, field goal and extra point. Four blank, 10-guage shotgun shells are fired in approval of the Horns. The Texas Cowboys are the keepers of Smokey, and they set the cannon off every time we score.

The mascot of the University of Texas, Bevo, a Longhorn steer, made his debut in 1916 during the 21-7 Texas win over Texas A&M. Stephen Pickney (1911) spearheaded a movement to provide a live mascot for the University of Texas, collecting $1.00 each from 124 alumni. On Thanksgiving Day, 1916, the frightened Bevo was dragged on to the field and formally presented to the students. The first mascot was branded by Aggies with "13-0" which was the score of the A&M victory the year before. A humiliated group of Texas students tried to save face by altering the numerals "13-0" to read "Bevo," the Longhorn name in the first place. ("Bevo" was the name of a popular beer made by Budweiser.)

Running the flag onto the field started on January 1, 1961 when the University of Texas played Mississippi in the Cotton Bowl. By request of Mississippi, a large Texas flag was made for their half-time show, so that they could salute the University of Texas and the state. Following the game, they presented the flag as a gift to Texas Governor Price Daniel who gave it to the Longhorn Band. The flag was so big, it was impossible for the band to handle, as well as participate in their own halftime activities, so he gave it to the Athletic Department. The Athletic Department then turned over all rights and operations of the flag to Alpha Phi Omega, a service fraternity. Today, the flag measures 45 by 25 yards and weighs 400 pounds. It is the largest Texas flag in the world. At the beginning of every home football game and at some out-of-town games, members of Alpha Phi Omega run the flag onto the field.

Lighting the Tower is tradition for UT Austin. The entire Tower is lit orange for a conference championship (Big XII Conference Championship), and an orange Tower with a number one signifies a national championship. The tower is also lit orange for special holidays, graduation ceremonies, and various other events. When Ricky Williams won the Heisman Trophy, the Tower was lit up with his number, 34. For graduation ceremonies the Tower is lit up with the graduation year.

Finding a Job or Internship

The Lowdown On...
Finding a Job or Internship

Every college has its own career center where you can get information about jobs and internships. Every major has an internship class, and some majors or colleges require internships for their students.

Advice

Try to do several internships while in college, as it will help you out once you have graduated. Internships give you contacts and valuable experience, as well as great people who can give you recommendations for future jobs or graduate school. The people who do internships are the ones who are more likely to find jobs when they graduate—sometimes with the companies they interned for, sometimes with other companies.

Career Center Resources & Services

http://www.utexas.edu/employment/students.html

Access UT Job Bank

Hire a Longhorn Job Bank

Career Exploration Center

Architecture Career Services

Business Career Services

Communication Career
Services

Education Career Services

Engineering Career Services

Fine Arts Career Services

Health Professions Office

Law School Career Services

Liberal Arts Career Services

Longhorn P.R.I.D.E. Progr

Natural Sciences Career
Services

Public Affairs Office of Student
and Alumni Programs

School of Information Career
Services

Social Work Career Services

Texas Exes Career Services

Average Salary Information

These are average salaries for the different colleges within the
University of Texas. It will obviously depend on what your specific
major is within each college, but with over 100 majors available,
it would be next to impossible to find the average salary of each
one. These are average entry-level salaries based on surveys of
recent UT graduates.

Architecture	$52.000
Business	$45,000
Communications	$29,000
Education	$25,000
Engineering	$49,000
Fine Arts	$23,000
Liberal Arts	$32,000
Natural Sciences	$39,000
Nursing	$45,000
Social Work	$31,000

Alumni

The Lowdown On...
Alumni

Web Site:
www.texasexes.org

Office:
2110 San Jacinto, in the
Alumni Center

Major Alumni Events:
Parent's Weekend,
Distinguished Alumnus
Awards, University of Texas
business network meetings,
Texas Exes chapter meetings,
Thirsty Thursdays, class
reunions, Pre- and Post-
football game gatherings at
the Alumni Center

Services Available:
Alumni directory, Alumni
Notes, Texas Orange Pages,
career network, permanent
e-mail forwarding, alumni
trips, pre-game activities at
the Alumni Center, career
services, career consultations
and assessments, career
seminars, continuing
education, Texas Exes
chapters around the world

Alumni Publications:
The Alcalde

Did You Know?

Famous UT Alums:

Bill Archer - politics
James A. Baker III - politics
Barbara Barrie - actress
Robert Benton - screenwriter
Lloyd Bentsen - politics
Dolph Briscoe - former Governor of Texas
Laura Bush - First Lady
Earl Campbell - football
Liz Carpenter - journalist
Tom C. Clark - Supreme Court Justice
Roger Clemens - baseball
Rita C. Clements - former First Lady of Texas
Joel Coen - writer/director
Dabney Coleman - actor
John B. Connally - Former Governor of Texas
Mrs. Nellie Connally - former First Lady of Texas
Denton A. Cooley - medicine
Barbara Conrad - opera singer
Margaret Cousins - author
Roy Crane - cartoonist
Ben Crenshaw - golfer
Robert L. Crippen - astronaut
Walter Cronkite - journalist
Mrs. Bing Crosby - actress
Michael Dell - computers
Lloyd Doggett - Senator
Edwin Dorn - politics
Ron Ely - actor
Don Evans - politics
Farrah Fawcett - actress
Peri Gilpin - actress
Marcia Gay Harden - actress
Shelby Hearon - author

Stephen Herek - director
Miss Ima Hogg - philanthropist
Karen Elliott House - journalist
Kay Bailey Hutchison - senator
Bobby R. Inman - military
Lady Bird Johnson - former First Lady
Janis Joplin - musician
Tom Kite - golfer
Tom Landry - football
Tom Loeffler - politics
Jayne Mansfield - actress
Red McCombs - business
Matthew McConaughey - actor
Bill Moyers - journalist
Tommy Nobis - football
Fess Parker - actor
Frederico Pena - politics
Mitch Pileggi - actor
Dan Rather - journalist
Sam Rayburn - Speaker of the House
Kevin Reynolds - director
Harvey Schmidt - composer
Alan Shivers - former Governor of Texas
Sheik Abdullah Tariki - co-founder of OPEC
Owen Temple - Texas country singer
Fernando Belaúnde Terry - former President of Peru
Rip Torn - actor
Tommy Tune - actor
Eli Wallach - actor
William S. White - author and columnist
Ricky Williams - football
Owen Wilson - actor
Ralph W. Yarborough - politics
Renee Zellweger - actress

Student Organizations

Student Organizations

There are more than 900 student organizations at the University of Texas, here are a few of the myriad of choices. View the entire list at *http://utdirect.utexas.edu/dsorg*

Sample Political Organizations: College Republicans at Texas, University Democrats, Students Against Cruelty to Animals, Students for Free Market Capitalism, Movimiento Estudiantil Chicana/o de Aztlan (MECHA), Libertarian Longhorns, Campus Greens

Sample Honorary Organizations: Order of Omega-Greek Honor Society, Alpha Phi Sigma-Pre Med, Mortar Board, Alpha Lambda Delta-Freshman Honor Society, Gamma Sigma Alpha-Greek Honor Society, National Society of Collegiate Scholars, Beta Beta Beta Biological Honor Society

Sample Student Governance Organizations: Undergraduate Business Council, Liberal Arts Council, Communication Council, San Jacinto Residence Hall Association, Student Government, Student Government Election Supervisory Board, Senate of College Councils, Student Bar Association

Sample Professional Organizations: Beta Alpha Rho-Pre Law Fraternity, R.O.I. (Return on Investment), Black Health Professions Organization, National Student Speech, Language and Hearing Organization

Sample Social Organizations: Pi Beta Phi, Pi Kappa Alpha, Silver Spurs, University Sailors, Texas Soccer Hooligans, Singer/Songwriter Alliance, Women's Law Caucus, Longhorn Hellraisers, Texas Six Shooters, Mullet, Texas Wranglers, Texas Cowboys, Frisbee Friends, Texas Matchmates

Sample Recreational Organizations: UT Cycling Sports Clubs, Longhorn Skiers, STEEL Dance Company, Skate Gang, University Chess Association, Wrestling Team

Sample Religious Organizations: Texas Wesley UMCM, Christian Coed, Pagan Student Alliance, Beta Upsilon Chi, Adventist Christian Fellowship, Korean Undergraduate Baptist Students, Presbyterian Campus Ministry

Sample Service Organizations: Silver Spurs, Texas Wranglers, Texas Cowboys, Alpha Phi Omega, Texas Lassos, Texas Rugby Little Sisters, American Red Cross Club at UT, Disch-Falk Diamonds, Orange Jackets, Dance Marathon, Texas Angels

Sample International/Cultural Organizations: Taiwanese American Students Association, Indian Cultural Association, Model United Nations, Campus Fusion, Mexican Students Association, CinemaTexas Short Film and Video Festival, African Students Association, Recording Artists Committee

Sample Special-Interest Organizations: Texas Travesty, Red Pill Forum, Dawson's Creek Club, Roustabouts Dance Company, Texas Knitters, Texas Sport Watching Club, Albino Squirrel Preservation Society, Student Health Advisory Committee (SHAC), Collegiate Leadership Council, Texas Exes Student Chapter, Dead Poets Society, Longhorn League of Gnomes, Men Against Sexual Assault, University Theater Guild, AlgoRhythms, The Ruthless Raiders, The Yellow Book

The Best & Worst

The Ten BEST Things About UT at Austin

1	Longhorn football
2	Wearing shorts and flip-flops all year
3	Good academics at a quality price
4	6th St. when you are 21+
5	Great alumni
6	Greek system
7	Bar on campus—Cactus Café
8	Basketball and baseball
9	The girls
10	Cheap drinks

The Ten **WORST** Things About UT at Austin

1	No parking
2	Heavy traffic
3	Cost of living
4	6th St. until you are 21
5	Drag rats
6	Foreign professors that you can't understand
7	Jester
8	The constant handing out of flyers on the West Mall
9	Theft
10	Protests

Visiting

The Lowdown On...
Visiting

Hotel Information:

Austin Folk House
506 W. 22nd St.
(866) 737-5019
Bed and Breakfast
Distance from Campus: Less
than one mile
Price Range: $109-$155
www.austinfolkhouse.com

Austins Inn at Pearl Street
809 W Martin Luther King Jr
Blvd
(800) 494-2261
Distance from Campus: Less
than one mile
Price Range: $89-$200
http://www.innpearl.com

Carriage House Inn
1110 W. 22 1/2 St.
(512) 472-2333
Distance from Campus: Less
than one mile
Price Range: $130-$150
www.carriagehouseinn.org

Carrington's Bluff Bed and Breakfast

1900 David St.

(512) 479-0638

Distance from Campus: Less than one mile

Price Range: $105-$159

http://carringtonsbluff.citysearch.com/

The Driskill

604 Brazos St.

(888) 507-5389

Distance from Campus: Less than two miles

Price Range: $195-$450

www.driskillhotel.com

Doubletree Club Hotel-University Area

1617 IH-35 North

(512)-479-4000

Distance from Campus: Less than one mile

Price Range: $139-$149

www.doubletree.com

Doubletree Guest Suites Hotel

303 W. 15th St.

(512) 478-7000

Distance from Campus: Less than one mile

Price Range: $116-$204

www.doubletree.com

Drury Inn and Suites Austin North

6711 I-35 N

(512) 467-9500

Distance from Campus: Less than five miles

Price Range: $80-$100

www.druryhotels.com

Governor's Inn

611 W. 22nd St.

(512) 477-0711

Bed and Breakfast

Distance from Campus: Less than one mile

Price Range: $99-$299

http://www.governorsinn.citysearch.com/

Hilton

500 East 4th St.

(512) 482-8000

Distance from Campus: Less than two miles

Price Range: $189-$214

www.hilton.com

Mansion at Judge's Hill

1900 Rio Grande

(800) 311-1619

Distance from Campus: Less than one mile

Price Range: $99-$299

www.mansionatjudgeshill.com

Take a Campus Virtual Tour

http://www.utexas.edu/tours/vrc

Schedule a Group Information Session

UT arranges special group visits for groups of 10 or more college-bound high school students. During these group visits, there are presentations by staff and students, as well as offer a tour of campus. Please call (512) 475-7440 ("schedule a visit for 10 or more people" option) at least two weeks before your group's desired visit date to schedule an appointment.

Campus Tours

High school juniors and seniors and their families are encouraged to visit the campus to learn more about UT. Staff at the Freshman Admissions Center will help arrange a campus visit to address your interests and needs as a prospective student. Please call (512) 475-7440 at least two weeks in advance to schedule an appointment.

The University also sponsors guided walking tours of the campus for non-college-bound visitors. These depart from the Information Desk on the ground floor of the Main Building (UT Tower). Tours are offered Monday through Saturday most of the year. Reservations are not required.

Overnight Visits

There are no specifically scheduled overnight visits, except for Longhorn Honors, which is for students who have been offered admission to the University. High school seniors who have been offered admission to UT are invited to an overnight stay and a full day of activities on campus. Prospective students will have the opportunity to interact with current UT students, faculty, and staff.

Directions to Campus

Driving from the North
Take I-35 South, exit MLK Blvd. Turn right on MLK, the Freshman Admissions Center will be on your left at MLK and Red River. Follow MLK to Guadalupe, Turn right and campus will be on your right.

Driving from the South
Take I-35 North, exit MLK Blvd. Turn Left on MLK, the Freshman Admissions Center will be on your left at MLK and Red River. Follow MLK to Guadalupe, Turn right and campus will be on your right

Driving from the East
Take 290 West to I-35 South, exit MLK Blvd. Turn right on MLK, the Freshman Admissions Center will be on your left at MLK and Red River. Follow MLK to Guadalupe, Turn right and campus will be on your right.

Driving from the West
Take 183 South to I-35 South, exit MLK Blvd. Turn right on MLK, the Freshman Admissions Center will be on your left at MLK and Red River. Follow MLK to Guadalupe, Turn right and campus will be on your right.

Words to Know

Academic Probation – A suspension imposed on a student if he or she fails to keep up with the school's minimum academic requirements. Those unable to improve their grades after receiving this warning can face dismissal.

Beer Pong / Beirut – A drinking game involving cups of beer arranged in a pyramid shape on each side of a table. The goal is to get a ping pong ball into one of the opponent's cups by throwing the ball or hitting it with a paddle. If the ball lands in a cup, the opponent is required to drink the beer.

Bid – An invitation from a fraternity or sorority to 'pledge' (join) that specific house.

Blue-Light Phone – Brightly-colored phone posts with a blue light bulb on top. These phones exist for security purposes and are located at various outside locations around most campuses. In an emergency, a student can pick up one of these phones (free of charge) to connect with campus police or a security escort.

Campus Police – Police who are specifically assigned to a given institution. Campus police are typically not regular city officers; they are employed by the university in a full-time capacity.

Club Sports – A level of sports that falls somewhere between varsity and intramural. If a student is unable to commit to a varsity team but has a lot of passion for athletics, a club sport could be a better, less intense option. Even less demanding, intramural (IM) sports often involve no traveling and considerably less time.

Cocaine – An illegal drug. Also known as "coke" or "blow," cocaine often resembles a white crystalline or powdery substance. It is highly addictive and dangerous.

Common Application – An application with which students can apply to multiple schools.

Course Registration – The period of official class selection for the upcoming quarter or semester. Prior to registration, it is best to prepare several back-up courses in case a particular class becomes full. If a course is full, students can place themselves on the waitlist, although this still does not guarantee entry.

Division Athletics – Athletic classifications range from Division I to Division III. Division IA is the most competitive, while Division III is considered to be the least competitive.

Dorm – A dorm (or dormitory) is an on-campus housing facility. Dorms can provide a range of options from suite-style rooms to more communal options that include shared bathrooms. Most first-year students live in dorms. Some upperclassmen who wish to stay on campus also choose this option.

Early Action – An application option with which a student can apply to a school and receive an early acceptance response without a binding commitment. This system is becoming less and less available.

Early Decision – An application option that students should use only if they are certain they plan to attend the school in question. If a student applies using the early decision option and is admitted, he or she is required and bound to attend that university. Admission rates are usually higher among students who apply through early decision, as the student is clearly indicating that the school is his or her first choice.

Ecstasy – An illegal drug. Also known as "E" or "X," ecstasy looks like a pill and most resembles an aspirin. Considered a party drug, ecstasy is very dangerous and can be deadly.

Ethernet – An extremely fast Internet connection available in most university-owned residence halls. To use an Ethernet connection properly, a student will need a network card and cable for his or her computer.

Fake ID – A counterfeit identification card that contains false information. Most commonly, students get fake IDs with altered birthdates so that they appear to be older than 21 (and therefore of legal drinking age). Even though it is illegal, many college students have fake IDs in hopes of purchasing alcohol or getting into bars.

Frosh – Slang for "freshman" or "freshmen."

Hazing – Initiation rituals administered by some fraternities or sororities as part of the pledging process. Many universities have outlawed hazing due to its degrading and sometimes dangerous nature.

Intramurals (IMs) – A popular, and usually free, sport league in which students create teams and compete against one another. These sports vary in competitiveness and can include a range of activities—everything from billiards to water polo. IM sports are a great way to meet people with similar interests.

Keg – Officially called a half-barrel, a keg contains roughly 200 12-ounce servings of beer.

LSD – An illegal drug. Also known as acid, this hallucinogenic drug most commonly resembles a tab of paper.

Marijuana – An illegal drug. Also known as weed or pot; along with alcohol, marijuana is one of the most commonly-found drugs on campuses across the country.

Major –The focal point of a student's college studies; a specific topic that is studied for a degree. Examples of majors include physics, English, history, computer science, economics, business, and music. Many students decide on a specific major before arriving on campus, while others are simply "undecided" until delcaring a major. Those who are extremely interested in two areas can also choose to double major.

Meal Block – The equivalent of one meal. Students on a meal plan usually receive a fixed number of meals per week. Each meal, or "block," can be redeemed at the school's dining facilities in place of cash. Often, a student's weekly allotment of meal blocks will be forfeited if not used.

Minor – An additional focal point in a student's education. Often serving as a complement or addition to a student's main area of focus, a minor has fewer requirements and prerequisites to fulfill than a major. Minors are not required for graduation from most schools; however some students who want to explore many different interests choose to pursue both a major and a minor.

Mushrooms – An illegal drug. Also known as "'shrooms," this drug resembles regular mushrooms but is extremely hallucinogenic.

Off-Campus Housing – Housing from a particular landlord or rental group that is not affiliated with the university. Depending on the college, off-campus housing can range from extremely popular to non-existent. Students who choose to live off campus are typically given more freedom, but they also have to deal with possible subletting scenarios, furniture, bills, and other issues. In addition to these factors, rental prices and distance often affect a student's decision to move off campus.

Office Hours – Time that teachers set aside for students who have questions about coursework. Office hours are a good forum for students to go over any problems and to show interest in the subject material.

Pledging – The early phase of joining a fraternity or sorority, pledging takes place after a student has gone through rush and received a bid. Pledging usually lasts between one and two semesters. Once the pledging period is complete and a particular student has done everything that is required to become a member, that student is considered a brother or sister. If a fraternity or a sorority would decide to "haze" a group of students, this initiation would take place during the pledging period.

Private Institution – A school that does not use tax revenue to subsidize education costs. Private schools typically cost more than public schools and are usually smaller.

Prof – Slang for "professor."

Public Institution – A school that uses tax revenue to subsidize education costs. Public schools are often a good value for in-state residents and tend to be larger than most private colleges.

Quarter System (or Trimester System) – A type of academic calendar system. In this setup, students take classes for three academic periods. The first quarter usually starts in late September or early October and concludes right before Christmas. The second quarter usually starts around early to mid–January and finishes up around March or April. The last academic quarter, or "third quarter," usually starts in late March or early April and finishes up in late May or Mid-June. The fourth quarter is summer. The major difference between the quarter system and semester system is that students take more, less comprehensive courses under the quarter calendar.

RA (Resident Assistant) – A student leader who is assigned to a particular floor in a dormitory in order to help to the other students who live there. An RA's duties include ensuring student safety and providing assistance wherever possible.

Recitation – An extension of a specific course; a review session. Some classes, particularly large lectures, are supplemented with mandatory recitation sessions that provide a relatively personal class setting.

Rolling Admissions – A form of admissions. Most commonly found at public institutions, schools with this type of policy continue to accept students throughout the year until their class sizes are met. For example, some schools begin accepting students as early as December and will continue to do so until April or May.

Room and Board – This figure is typically the combined cost of a university-owned room and a meal plan.

Room Draw/Housing Lottery – A common way to pick on-campus room assignments for the following year. If a student decides to remain in university-owned housing, he or she is assigned a unique number that, along with seniority, is used to determine his or her housing for the next year.

Rush – The period in which students can meet the brothers and sisters of a particular chapter and find out if a given fraternity or sorority is right for them. Rushing a fraternity or a sorority is not a requirement at any school. The goal of rush is to give students who are serious about pledging a feel for what to expect.

Semester System – The most common type of academic calendar system at college campuses. This setup typically includes two semesters in a given school year. The fall semester starts around the end of August or early September and concludes before winter vacation. The spring semester usually starts in mid-January and ends in late April or May.

Student Center/Rec Center/Student Union – A common area on campus that often contains study areas, recreation facilities, and eateries. This building is often a good place to meet up with fellow students; depending on the school, the student center can have a huge role or a non-existent role in campus life.

Student ID – A university-issued photo ID that serves as a student's key to school-related functions. Some schools require students to show these cards in order to get into dorms, libraries, cafeterias, and other facilities. In addition to storing meal plan information, in some cases, a student ID can actually work as a debit card and allow students to purchase things from bookstores or local shops.

Suite – A type of dorm room. Unlike dorms that feature communal bathrooms shared by the entire floor, suites offer bathrooms shared only among the suite. Suite-style dorm rooms can house anywhere from two to ten students.

TA (Teacher's Assistant) – An undergraduate or grad student who helps in some manner with a specific course. In some cases, a TA will teach a class, assist a professor, grade assignments, or conduct office hours.

Undergraduate – A student in the process of studying for his or her bachelor's degree.

ABOUT THE AUTHOR

Writing this book was one of the most fun things I have ever undertaken. I never thought of myself as a writer, per se, but I did know that I knew more than most people about the University of Texas. If I could make a career out of being a UT student, I definitely would, because my time here has unquestionably been the best years of my life.

I grew up in The Woodlands, Texas, graduated from Woodlands High School, and I came to UT. I completed my Bachelor of Science in radio-television-film, then finished my Bachelor of Science in communication studies with an emphasis in human relations. I also completed a business foundations minor and a concentration in psychology. While at Texas, I was a member of Pi Beta Phi sorority, and I enjoyed volunteering at the Children's Hospital of Austin among other projects. I am currently still living in Austin, and I'm not in a hurry to leave. If anyone wants to contact me with questions or comments about anything, feel free, at erinhall@collegeprowler.com.

Now that I am finished with this book, it is back to the job search, so if anyone wants to hire me, feel free to do that, as I am available. I would like to thank the people who helped me with this book: Meredith, Courtney, Mom, Kyle—thanks for always answering my questions, Rhodes, Drew, Lindsay S., Jordan, Dustin, Cameron, Alex, Focker, Tim Grahh, Tay Tay, Robert, Gavin, Michelle, Marisa, Mark, Michael Paul, Liberty, all of the Pike boys—I love y'all. Special thanks to Trey and Callaway for letting me constantly bother them, and the biggest thanks to Lindsay Hale, my personal editor, for her amazing help on this book. I couldn't have done it without you.

I would like to dedicate this book to a friend whom we lost too soon. She should have been here at UT enjoying these years with me and everyone else who loved her.

This book is dedicated to:
Meghan Manning 2/2/80-5/6/97
I'm sure she's doing a "Hook 'em Horns" up in Heaven.

Erin Hall